Across the Severn

D1610182

2000562530

NEATH PORT TALBOT LIBRARIES

ACROSS THE SEVERN

Migration of a Welsh family

NEATH PORT TALBOT LIBRARIES

EVA GOLDSWORTHY

y Lolfa

NEATH PORT TALBOT
LIBRARIES

CL.   942. 082

DATE 29/07/09   PR. 6·95

LOC   Pon

NO 2000562530

First impression: 2009

© Eva Goldsworthy & Y Lolfa Cyf., 2009

*This book is subject to copyright
and may not be reproduced by any means
except for review purposes
without the prior written consent of the publishers.*

Cover design: Y Lolfa

ISBN: 9781847711175

Printed on acid-free and partly recycled paper
and published and bound in Wales by
Y Lolfa Cyf., Talybont, Ceredigion SY24 5AP
e-mail ylolfa@ylolfa.com
website www.ylolfa.com
tel 01970 832 304
fax 832 782

ACKNOWLEDGEMENT

This scamper through the twentieth century began as a tribute to my parents May and Joe Goldsworthy and their lives in the Ogmore and Severn valleys, but as it progressed I found that I myself was drawn into it as an unwilling participant. In contrast to May and Joe's awesome courage in leaving Wales for an uncertain future, my early life was largely unsuccessful and I must have been a disappointment to them. For example, I refused to go to a university, I can't play the piano (I didn't practise) and I turned down the opportunity to learn to ride a horse. Ironically it is only since their deaths that my life has become more positive – too late, unfortunately, for their approbation.

*Dedicated to my three daughters, whose encouragement
and generosity helped to make this book possible*

CHAPTER 1

A Child in Wales

(With apologies to Dylan Thomas)

" GOLDSWORTHY! THAT'S AN unusual name," said the English doctor to my father.

"It's Cornish," said Joe. "I had a Cornish father and a Welsh mother."

"And a damn good mixture!" replied Dr Haines.

But this was long after we had left the valley.

The Welsh valleys lie in the north/south corrugations of the South Wales coal fields. Over the ages, water from the Brecon Beacons and the Black Mountains made deep troughs as it flowed down to the sea. In these troughs lie valley towns such as Pontypridd, Treorchy, Treharris, Pontilanfraith, Ystradgynlais and Ogmore.

There were only three miles between the small Welsh town of Ogmore Vale and the village of Blackmill, but as I walked along with my parents, holding my father's hand, the distance seemed endless to my stocky three-year-old legs. We started from our house in Bryn Road in Ogmore, then went down to Walters Road, alongside the railway crossing and on to the tarmac.

"This is the road to Bridgend," said my father as we walked on past the steeply-pitched cemetery with its slate headstones.

"Aren't we going to Grandpa's?" I asked in alarm. "I thought they asked us to tea!"

Mam laughed. "And that's where we are going, *cariad*; Blackmill is only on the way to Bridgend. You wouldn't want to walk that far now, would you?!"

I was very relieved. At that time I had very little conception of distance, but as I had done the journey several times before, I knew that the tramp to Blackmill was my limit and that the town of Bridgend was a world away. The journey was always interesting; the bare mountains on either side making us feel small and insignificant walking along below them, and when we stepped out from the smut and grime of Ogmore into the clean air of the countryside, I was again fascinated by the change in the appearance of the sheep. In Ogmore they were grey and speckled with soot from the local colliery, but by the time we got to Lewistown, a small hamlet between Ogmore and Blackmill, they were already looking more like the sheep in my picture books. By the time we had got as far as the Glynogwr turning and swung down into Blackmill proper, the surrounding hills were dotted with snow-white fluffs of wool.

It was only when I grew older I realised that the difference between Ogmore and Blackmill lay deep underground and it consisted of gold – black gold. No coal had been discovered beneath Blackmill's bare hills and lush meadows, but in Ogmore a spur from the seams in the Rhondda Valley had pushed towards the town and a mine had been constructed at Nant-y-moel called the Wyndham Western Colliery. Ogmore was grey compared to Blackmill; after a shower the streets ran with dirty rivulets, the sheep on the mountains were peppered with black specks and the miners coming off a shift were grey with coal dust (there were no pit baths in those days). There is a sketch by Welsh stand-up comedian Max Boyce about a small boy who is asked by his teacher to make a crayon drawing of his home. "What colour is the valley, Mam?" he asks. She answers, "Rhondda grey."

This abrupt change in the landscape was a normal phenomenon at that time in Wales. There must have been coal throughout the Rhondda, Llangeinwyr, Garw and Ogmore valleys, but only a few pockets were developed. Why had Wales not followed the blanket industrialisation of the Midlands? Were the coal owners less astute? Was the population too thinly spread? Was Wales too far away, with an alien language? Were the speculators short of cash? Whatever the reason, the familiar winding gear of the collieries never dominated the Welsh skyline as much as the chimney stacks of the Black Country.

These questions did not of course bother my young mind as we arrived at last at Heatherville, the house by the river in Blackmill where the Goldsworthy family lived after moving from Ty'n y Graig (the stone house), a farmstead further up the valley. The tea was laid out in the best parlour and I was given a piano stool to sit on with a cushion on top so that I could reach the plate of home-baked scones.

Early in the twentieth century Blackmill had been a busy little village with a flannel factory, a pub, a chapel, a railway halt and a signal box. At the end of the 1914/18 war a memorial was erected with the names of the dozen local boys who had been killed. The memorial was beside the bridge which spanned the shallow River Ogwr, and as I learned to carefully spell out the names, tracing them with my finger – Rich-ard Jones, El-wyn Proth-eroe – I used to wonder if the sound of the ripples over the stones was the last memory for some of them as they died.

By my time, the flannel factory had gone and a row of council houses had been built on the site next to the chapel, but Welsh flannel is hardwearing and my uncle David still wore shirts which had been made there. As a child I marvelled at my grandmother's smooth unwrinkled skin and put it down to the face flannels she used. They were made from the tails of Uncle Dai's old shirts, so I cajoled her to let me have one and I kept it for years, even though my skin never achieved the same smooth texture of my elderly grandmother.

My father Joseph (Joe) Goldsworthy was born in Blackmill; he and his twin brother Jim were from a family of nine living children, seven of them boys. Their father, William Henry, was a stone mason and an immigrant from Cornwall. He had been sent from Redruth to help build the great pillars of the viaduct which dominated the village, and he lodged with the Lewis family. It was there that he met Gwen, the daughter of the house, and married her. Gwen was an indomitable woman who supplemented the family income by running a shop in the village which had originally belonged to her brother Moses Lewis, and with the money it generated she tried to keep her sons out of the mine. But inevitably the lure of good employment had spread from Ogmore to Blackmill and most families had sons who preferred to work in the pit at Nant-y-moel than in poorly paid farming. Gwen tried to buck the trend by helping her oldest son Simon to start a farm; she bought the next one, David, a milk round and George, who had bad eyesight, was wangled a job on the railway, running the local signal box. Unfortunately, by the time the twins Joe and Jim left school at fourteen the shop wasn't doing too well and she had to give in and let them go down the mine.

"I hear you're good with horses, young man," said the colliery manager to Joe, referring to his habit of leaping bareback on to the wild ponies that roamed the hills.

"Yes sir," said Joe.

"We like to encourage initiative, so we will put you to train with a farrier and you can help manage the pit ponies."

So Joe served his apprenticeship and became a farrier to the ponies who lived and worked far underground in the dark, pulling the coal drams. He often compared their lot to the lives of their untamed brothers on the hills who were yet to be caught and broken in during the annual round-ups, but the new century was hard on people as well as animals so he accepted that their lifestyle was inevitable.

Unfortunately, Joe's twin brother Jim entered the mine as an ordinary collier and one dreadful day he was injured in an accident at the coal face and died later in a Bridgend hospital. A plaque in Paran Baptist Chapel (since removed in 1989 when the Evangelists took over) was all that remained of him. As a child I was told that "a bell fell on him," but that might have been a euphemism for the rather ghastly way some miners died.

Although he seldom mentioned it, the death of his twin marked my father for the rest of his life and probably contributed to his eventual decision to leave Wales. Jim's death was made even more poignant by the fact that the young man was already engaged to a local girl called Blodwen Roberts. She eventually became a schoolteacher and taught some of the younger Goldsworthies in the village school, but for some reason the family never acknowledged her after the accident. This was similar to the treatment that was meted out to my own mother years later when she began going out with my father. Blodwen never forgot her true love and for the rest of her life his memory brought tears to her eyes.

The three Goldsworthy girls in Heatherville – Gwenllyan,

Matilda and Miriam – were given schooling up to the age of fourteen but were then expected to either work in the shop, help with the housework or 'go into service'. Gwen went to work for what passed as the only 'big house' in the area which belonged to the Llewellyns – a local family which had done well running a general store in Ogmore – and she eventually became their chief cook. There was no class division in South Wales of the sort that still persisted in England, for being a country that had been occupied for six hundred years, Wales had no tradition of landed gentry. There was, however, a general dislike of the occupier, but the people who ran the store in Ogmore were local, so Grandmother Goldsworthy felt no shame that her daughter Gwen was working for them.

Unfortunately, the second unmarried daughter Matilda became pregnant, which could spell disaster in such a straight-laced Baptist village. It normally meant being sent to the workhouse in Bridgend where, six weeks after the birth, the baby would be removed from the mother, as such women were seen as unfit to take on the responsibility of raising a child. Here again, Grandmother Goldsworthy took control and by some alchemy she managed to convince the neighbours that the baby was hers. How she did it I can't imagine, because the only photograph I have of her shows a tiny woman with a tiny waist. Only the eldest son Simon realised what was going on and he was sworn to secrecy. Sadly, Matilda died at the comparatively young age of thirty-six, probably because the strain of living with her own child and not being able to acknowledge it had a terrible effect on her.

Miriam, the third daughter, married young to Ernest Keylock who was a farm labourer in Coity, but they later moved to a council house in Bridgend. My parents and I rarely went to visit them and I felt that there was a tacit assumption that living in a council house had dented the family's pride. Maybe I picked up this idea from my mother who, bless her, was inclined to innocent delusions of grandeur.

The Goldsworthy family was large, even by Victorian standards. Where did that clutch of children sleep before the older ones began to peel off and set up on their own? One clue was the large corrugated iron shed in the yard at the back of the house. It almost filled the available space and rested on a base made of railway sleepers, so that one had to walk up steps to get into it. I remember those steps; to a three-year-old they seemed impossibly high and there was no rail to hang on to. The shed was open plan inside and contained a tin bath, a kitchen section with a paraffin stove and a space left for bunks. The paraffin stove was only used as an auxiliary for the principal cooking operation which took place in the main room of the house on a large coal-burning range. This was polished to mirror-like blackness with 'Zebra' – a lead-based polish which grandmother sold in the shop. The range served to heat the water, bake cakes and cook meat, and with the aid of a 'Dutch oven' (a horizontal grill fixed to the front bars of the fire) turned out meals for the whole Goldsworthy clan.

This main room was furnished with a large table, some hardback chairs and the traditional Welsh sideboard. The china on it was arranged decoratively but was never put to everyday use, and the top shelf was reserved for a dozen brass candlesticks of varying heights. I pondered long on the arrangement of those candlesticks; to my young eyes they were very high up and I used to wonder if instead of being in ascending order they could be set more symmetrically about the middle. (Maybe this was the beginning of my abiding interest in mathematics, culminating in a hard-won degree as a mature student – but that's another story.) The candlesticks were of course highly polished, as was the furniture – even the cheap linoleum which covered the floors and the stairs was buffed to such a degree that you could see your face in it.

Beside the range there was an airy walk-in pantry where the perishable foodstuffs were kept (no fridges in those days). Sides of bacon hung from hooks fixed to the ceiling, and Grandmother would slice some off for breakfast or dinner. Her daughter, my auntie Gwen, who had moved to Ogmore when she married Uncle Jim Jones, also had a walk-in pantry, but it wasn't big enough to hang sides of bacon. I used to wonder how she managed to feed her family with no bacon as a standby. "Auntie Gwen buys her bacon from John the butcher's shop in Ogmore," explained my mother when I asked her. My first understanding of commerce!

The remaining room on the ground floor was the front parlour, which was only used on special occasions such as funerals and Sunday teas. It had the obligatory piano found in every Welsh home, and dark oak furniture. The focus of the room was the heavy Welsh Bible. It lay on a table, open at the page where names of all the members of the family were inscribed. It was rarely read because the strictures against the Welsh language were already beginning to bite. Welsh was forbidden in the schools, and Welshmen who couldn't speak English were not allowed to take up public office. All newspapers and official forms were in English and the indigenous language was only allowed in the Nonconformist chapels. In the Goldsworthy family the older children, Simon, George and Gwen, were fluent Welsh speakers, but the other girls and the three younger boys, David, Joe and Jim, less so. For the first three years of my life I learnt to speak English heavily larded with Welsh words, but even these disappeared when we went to England and I have now lost the language completely. But I have a fond memory of Auntie Gwen telling me how to pronounce '*os gwelwch yn dda*' (please)!

An added nail in the coffin of *Iaith Gymraeg* (Welsh language) in South Wales was the influx of foreigners, including, of course, my Cornish grandfather, William Henry. The Cornish were mostly recruited for the mines or as stone masons, while the Irish worked mainly on building sites. There was even a sprinkling of Italian ice-cream sellers throughout the valleys! The Cornish tin mines had been operational since the times of the ancient Phoenicians, those early navigators and traders from present-day Lebanon, but the mines were now in decline, with disused towers and engine houses dotting the skyline. The Welsh coal industry, on the other hand, was thriving and needed experienced men. When they arrived in Wales, the Cornishmen soon adapted to digging for coal because the principles of the two types of mining were very similar: shoring up tunnels with pit props, wielding picks, ensuring ventilation and guarding against gas and flooding. I imagine the Cornish were particularly wary of flooding because back home they were used to following tin seams far out under the sea. Due to their common Celtic roots, the Welsh were not as antagonistic towards the Cornish and Irish as they were to the English. Nevertheless, since English was the principal means of communication between the races, the local language became further diluted.

The whole Goldsworthy family had somehow been accommodated in Heatherville with the help of the outside shed, but by the time I knew it the exodus had already started. Simon was a part-time collier and also ran a farm at Hendre Post (the old post office), Jim had been killed in the mine, my father Joseph had married and moved to Ogmore, both

Miriam and Gwen were married, and unhappy Matilda had died unmarried in 1923. Cornish grandfather William Henry, a stonemason who had been recruited by the GWR to build the viaduct in Blackmill, had already passed away having succumbed to the disease of pneumoconiosis, but as he was a mason it was due to stone dust rather than coal dust. Now all that were left in Heatherville were my widowed grandmother and her sons George, David and William, so there was plenty of room in the house. Once, however, my parents stayed overnight and I was obliged to share a bed with my grandmother. She slept in flannelette sheets and the heat from them made me come out in spots.

Long before I was thought of and when he was still an apprentice, my father managed to go to classes at the Workmen's Hall in Ogmore. These places of recreation and learning had been set up all over the coalfields by the miners themselves contributing a penny a week from their wages. Joe hadn't had the opportunity to go to a grammar school but he still knew that there was a whole world out there beyond the Welsh mountains. At the Workmen's Hall he listened to lectures on human biology, the physical sciences and modern history. He read about Tom Paine and Garibaldi, and in the modest library there was a copy of union leader Noel Ablett's recent book advocating the nationalisation of the coal industry. He also went to a meeting in Merthyr in the Rhondda where the radical Scot Kier Hardie had been surprisingly elected Mayor. Joe's idol was Mahatma Gandhi, the Indian nationalist, and he was fascinated by this puny little man who had the strength to face up to the whole of the British Empire.

There were Workmen's Halls in every town in South Wales and they did much to radicalise the people against the existing order. Some called these halls 'hot beds of dissent', but they did a lot of good in advocating change. Together with the chapels they gave people hope for a future which lay beyond the daily trudge to the pit and the weary return covered with coal dust, which remained ingrained in the skin even after the ritual scrub in a tin bath by the fire. I have always been able to spot a miner by the slivers of coal which remain indelibly lodged in his hands.

The paradox of the miner is that, although he is fiercely proud of his calling, he does his best to prevent his sons following it. The principal escape route was through education, and even now at the beginning of the twenty-first century a disproportionate number of teachers from Wales migrate to England and work for the ILEA (Inner London Education Authority), several of my cousins among them. In Joe's time teaching qualifications were hard to come by, even though his tutor at the Workmen's Hall was heard to remark: "Young Goldsworthy has the makings of a prominent man." In Wales, 'prominent' was code for 'public' which was itself a further code for 'socialist'. Socialism took a hold in the valleys of South Wales more easily than in the rest of the British Isles because it was already a classless society, and Joe might have been groomed for political life had not events far from home intervened.

CHAPTER 2

Violet May Edwards

M Y MOTHER, VIOLET May Edwards, came from
Ogmore Vale which was distinctly urban compared
to Blackmill. The population lived in rows of identical back-
to-back houses which followed the contours of the hills on
the high ground and the twists of the River Ogwr (Ogmore)
on the low ground. My mother's family lived in the top part
of the town which gave them a view of the whole valley
extending as far as the pit at Nant-y-moel, so from infancy she
was accustomed to seeing the night shift stepping from their
cage and trudging homewards, some with sawn-off chunks
of pit props under their arms. They were tired and dragged
their feet, and their face and hands were blackened with coal
dust which was accentuated by the white circles round their
eyes. They had worked a cramped twelve-hour shift in the
dark mine but as they came up into the morning sunshine
their spirits lifted and one or two began to sing. Soon a dozen
or more were harmonising and the hymns they had learnt in
the Primitive Methodist Chapel by the river echoed from the
surrounding hills.

No one thought to question the ethics of obliging all able
men to spend the best hours of their lives underground in
the dark, and this morning ritual seemed as normal to my
mother as any other daily event in the valley – the women
on their knees scrubbing their doorsteps, the tin bath hanging
on a nail waiting to be filled with water from the coal range,

the occasional sheep wandering down from the hills and rummaging in dustbins, and the off-duty miner squatting on his haunches in the sunshine outside his front door.

As befitted a 'metropolis', Ogmore had a row of shops on high ground above the river. It was accessed by a steep hill called 'John the butcher's' because his was the first shop in the row. Further along there was a bakery, a men's outfitters and the *Gwalia*, a general store which was owned by the same Llewellyn family that Gwen Goldsworthy worked for as a cook. (This shop achieved fame half a century later by being transported stone by stone to be rebuilt at St Fagans, a site just outside Cardiff which has been set up to represent a Welsh village at the turn of the nineteenth century.) Finally, apart from the chapel and the Workman's Hall, the other notable building in Ogmore was the cinema, which doubled as a theatre for events such as a visiting male voice choir. One memorable visit was from a choir which had won the Crown at a recent national Eisteddfod.

My mother's father, Thomas Edwards, was from Blaenavon. Thomas wasn't a miner but a white-collar man and had worked as a clerk in the local colliery. He was a widower but then married a local girl, Elizabeth Jane Watkins, in 1891. Soon after the marriage he was transferred by the colliery owners to be a clerk at their colliery in Ogmore. Although the two towns were separated by thirty tortuous miles, the cement which held the valleys together – coal-mining and chapel – ensured that their move was painless.

The Edwards were comfortably well-off thanks to Thomas's salary and the rents from a house in Porth in the Rhondda Valley which Elizabeth Jane had brought as a dowry. The family was small compared to the Goldsworthies. Thomas and Elizabeth had four children: Tom, my mother

Violet May (known simply as May), Millie and Ivy. May was her father's favourite and he would often ask her: "Like to come over the *bwlch* with me, Puss?" when he went to Porth to collect the rents, and the two would climb over the pass of the high mountain which divided the Ogmore Valley from the one next door.

May went to school in Ogmore and enjoyed it, especially play time when she and her friends would rush up high above the school yard where a smooth piece of granite jutted out from the sheep-cropped grass. It was called 'the picky rock' and they slid down it with carefree abandon, so much so that more than once May went home with holes in her knickers. Was this a female version of Joe and his friends leaping on wild ponies?

When May was sent to a secretarial college in Cardiff, her mother insisted that she did not let the side down in the big city and kitted her out with the best that the Gwalia could provide. She had a new gabardine skirt with a matching jacket and a white shirt-blouse. These, with a wide hat, white cotton gloves and her calf-high leather boots satisfied my grandmother that May could hold her own in that sinful place several mountains away.

May did very well in college, showing what proved to be a life-long business acumen, perhaps inherited from her father the colliery clerk. Unfortunately she was recalled home before the end of the course, just when she was beginning to think that she might stay on in Cardiff and get a clerical job. Her mother had become seriously ill and May was needed to look after her young sisters. "Madness," said her tutor, annoyed at losing a star pupil, "it's madness." But in 1912 careers for girls were not taken seriously and May's hopes were dashed for the sake of the family back home. (A similar thing happened to a Goldsworthy cousin called Ceinwen who was at Ogmore Grammar. The headmaster was shattered when she was removed from school to look after younger siblings.) Typical of the time, the career of May's brother Tom, who spent his days messing about with the new-fangled science of electricity, was not affected.

May dutifully knuckled down and looked after her sick mother and her younger sisters but she didn't enjoy it. Her ailing mother had been a good cook but the genes hadn't been passed on, so she concentrated on the only item she felt capable of producing – *cawl cennin* (leek soup) – until the family rebelled and she was forced to diversify. She alleviated the dullness of her enforced domestic life by devoting her meagre spare time to activities in the chapel by the river, the 'Prim'. Throughout her life, almost up to the day that she died, she would sing the hymns that she had learnt by rote because she knew very little Welsh. Although her voice was untrained, it was clear and untrammelled against the background valley noises of bleating sheep and the whirr of the colliery mechanism.

While May played the role of the obedient daughter, the rest of the family didn't follow suit. Perhaps they thought that one saint in the family was sufficient. As for the others, Tom was immersed in wires and terminals and batteries, Millie ran away to work in the Pump Room in Llandrindod Wells and Ivy married a handsome but impecunious Irishman.

Eventually, my grandmother died and Thomas was left a widower. I remember him as an Old Testament figure with a beard, who gave me a whistle which I treasured for many years until I lost it in the family's move to England. He died ten years after his wife and was placed next to her in the sloping cemetery with its slate headstones. May, Tom and

Ivy, with husband Pat in tow, moved from the roomy house high up on the south side of the river to a small terrace in Walters Road in the valley. With her parents dead and her siblings more or less grown up, my mother realised that at last she was free to resume her interrupted life. What would she do with that freedom? Go back to college? Travel? Get married?

As with Joe, events far beyond the sheep and the winding gear on the Welsh skyline were to affect her decision. On 28 June 1914 the Archduke Franz Ferdinand was assassinated in Sarajevo, and on 4 August that same year Britain declared war on Germany.

CHAPTER 3

War Service

M Y PARENTS WERE both in their twenties when the 'War Against the Kaiser' broke out. According to official propaganda it fostered an unprecedented outbreak of patriotism fuelled by a spirit of adventure and a duty to defend the Empire. (When I was at school in the late twenties we were still commemorating Empire Day.) In the words of Rupert Brook, our young men became "swimmers into cleanness leaping." But the reality was a little different from that painted by the politicians and an over-enthusiastic poet.

In 1914 there were certainly thousands of volunteers and they joined up for diverse reasons, but many enlisted to avoid the grinding poverty of both the rural areas and the cities. This poverty was worrying the Establishment, already edgy with memories of the French Revolution, and it was whispered that the war came just in time to stop the British going down the same route. Certainly, revolution was in the air at the beginning of the twentieth century. Michael Collins in Ireland was agitating for Home Rule, Mahatma Gandhi had launched his civil disobedience campaign against the British Raj and the African colonies were beginning to become restive. In Britain there were home-grown socialists like Manny Shinwell and Kier Hardie preaching equality on street corners, while waiting in the wings was a sixteen-year-old Welshman filling coal drams deep in a Tredegar mine; his name was Aneurin Bevan. Yes, the 1914 war might have come just in time to prevent a revolution, but it only delayed the eventual unravelling of the privileged part of society which had built up during the previous decades.

Blackmill and Ogmore were lucky with regard to the war. When conscription eventually came, forced on the country by the terrible losses in the battles of the Somme and Passchendaele, miners and farmers were exempt. This applied to most of the men in the two communities, but of course individuals could volunteer and many did, including my father Joseph. Did he succumb to the famous poster (far ahead of its time) with the finger pointing aggressively forwards and the words: 'Kitchener Needs You'? Joseph joined a cavalry regiment – the 15th King's Hussars – and was immediately sent to France to serve as a farrier.

My uncle David was not exempt, his milk-round not being classified as vital to the war effort, but being antagonistic to all types of authority he ignored the call-up papers. Two military policemen came one morning and arrested him when he was on his way to Glynogwr with the milk churns. (I wonder what happened to the pony and cart?) They took him to Bridgend and put him in jail, but I was never told the end of the story. Maybe he became a conscientious objector, maybe none of the services wanted to take on such an awkward customer, or perhaps Grandmother Goldsworthy pulled off another of her tricks. I was not alive at the time but in later years when I encountered my Uncle Dai, I realised that he was still as bloody minded as he had been with relation to the call-up. By then he was a station master and a part-time postman delivering mail to Blackmill and the surrounding farms. "You see, Eva," he told me, "if I've got a stupid circular, I never bother to trudge up the mountain to deliver it."

When the British entered the 1914–18 war they did not

know what to expect; some even thought that it would be over by Christmas. Their most recent experience had been the Boer War in South Africa which had only ended twelve years previously. This had been fought on the other side of the world and had only involved several thousand men. It had been a mobile war entailing skirmishes with the Boer guerrillas over the vast expanses of the Orange Free State and the Transvaal. The war against the Kaiser turned out to be very different, more like the traditional sort of conflict where standing armies confronted each other head on. It was also fought on Britain's doorstep. After a few backward and forward offences it became tragically static. Opposite sides shot at each other from water-logged trenches trying to break each other's lines and from time to time the Generals made disastrous thrusts wasting thousands of men. "Lions led by donkeys," as the historian Alan Clark put it; and the following poem by one of those lions, Siegfried Sassoon, sums up the profligacy of those war years.

The General

"Good-morning; good-morning!" the General said
When we met him last week on our way to the line.
Now the soldiers he smiled at are most of 'em dead,
And we're cursing his staff for incompetent swine.
"He's a cheery old card," grunted Harry to Jack
As they slogged up to Arras with rifle and pack.
But he did for them both by his plan of attack.

Over those dreadful years the British and the Germans alike lost countless soldiers, immolated in the mud of Flanders, and when the war came to an end in November 1918 due to exhaustion on both sides, the returning men were disillusioned and tight lipped because their experience of trench warfare had been too awful to articulate. I only once heard my father mention anything about the actual conflict. He described what he had seen when his unit came to a wood in which a British battalion had been under heavy shell fire: "Pieces of men and horses hanging from the trees." His portable forge was just behind the front lines and it was there that he shod his beloved horses. I imagined him soothing them when he lifted a hoof on to his leather apron, some of them still shuddering from the noise of the incessant bombardment.

Although women were not yet conscripted, my mother used her new-found freedom to join the Royal Flying Corps, and I have a photograph of her looking very smart in her uniform. She had a belted greatcoat with lapels, a khaki skirt and shirt, woollen stockings, a collar and tie, a peaked cap on her head with the RFC insignia, and for a final touch, very airman-like gauntlet gloves. The photograph does not show anything of her waist-long hair; it must have been stuffed out of sight under the peaked cap, rather like the West Indian Rastafarians stuff their dreadlocks under their bonnets nowadays. Her uniform was a khaki colour – blue only being introduced much later when the Royal Flying Corps was changed to the Royal Air Force. May was twenty at the time and her father was loath to lose his favourite daughter, but showing the determination which persisted throughout her life she insisted, and I believe in the end he became very proud of her. Although subsequent events – marriage, children, business ventures – tended to blot out that earlier unique experience, I was gratified when she was invited to a service in Westminster Abbey to commemorate the sixtieth anniversary of the RFC. The 81-year-old May, ever impressed by royalty, was able to meet the Queen Mother and Princess Alice, Duchess of Gloucester.

May volunteered in the spirit of serving anywhere she was needed, but she ended up in Blandford Camp in Wiltshire. The camp was not an airfield but a transit depot where overseas airmen were processed before being sent to France. They had learnt to fly in Canada, Australia and White South Africa in the ramshackle aeroplanes of the day, and had come to England to fight for the Empire. Unlike Joe, May had no memories of carnage because the air battles took place on the other side of the channel. She was also spared the agony of seeing crippled planes coming back to base in France after a sortie over enemy lines, with the aircrew trying to stagger out before their flimsy machine burst into flames.

Blandford was rather like a boarding school, especially as it had many rules and regulations which were seen as a challenge to its inmates, even though breaking them might mean a court martial. The sexes weren't supposed to mix and there was a barbed wire fence separating them, but this wasn't sufficient to prevent clandestine meetings. When I was a child I loved hearing the stories my mother used to tell me at bed-time of pyjama parties and midnight feasts. She also delighted in describing a martinet female officer who had served with the women in France where conditions were tougher than in England. This woman tried to impose similar strictures on the girls at Blandford, but they rebelled and refused to eat the dry biscuits with which they had been served for breakfast. Instead they piled them up in a pyramid in the centre of the table. "Come on girls," said the ringleader, "let's show them what we think of their dog biscuits!" These were all feisty women who had cracked the gender code by joining up.

The 'war to end war' didn't end before Christmas. It

carried on for four weary years, or to put it bluntly, ground to a halt with neither side having gained anything significant. The soldiers came home to what was supposed to be the 'land fit for heroes' that Prime Minister David Lloyd George had promised, but somehow the promise never materialised. The West was bankrupt after the long war, especially Germany, due to the iniquitously harsh reparations that had been imposed on her at the Treaty of Versailles – the first acorn which took root and created the twisted oak of Nazism. In England the men came back to poverty and unemployment but in Wales at least, the miners had jobs to return to.

CHAPTER 4

Marriage
and a Coal Strike

WHAT DID MAY and Joe think of Wales after having been away so long? As far as I can make out they both accepted their lot and tried to make a go of life as they found it. For a brief period Joe considered going to Canada and joining the Canadian Mounted Police but nothing came of it, and I often wonder if his meeting with May influenced his change of plan. In any event, he went back to the Wyndham Colliery, thankful for a job after his stint in the army, and May returned to help her father run the family home.

But of course time had not stood still in the valleys. The war had broken down many barriers, and Ogmore and Blackmill were much more integrated. May soon got bored with being just a house daughter and again devoted her spare time to the two Nonconformist chapels, the Primitive Methodist in Ogmore and Paran Baptist in Blackmill. She took Sunday School classes and even preached a little, and when she got married and eventually left for England she was presented with a gold brooch in the form of a C and an E intertwined, denoting 'Christian Endeavour'. I have it still. My father, meanwhile, found little in common with his fellow workers whose contribution to the war effort, although valuable, had been in staying at home and producing coal. He continued his interrupted studies at the Workmen's Hall and was beginning to make plans for a political future.

Where did my parents meet and what did they say? Was it at a dance in that same Workmen's Hall, or was it walking 'over the *bwlch*' with friends? Wherever it was, they must have sensed their 'otherness', both of them having left the valleys and now seeing them in a fresh light. They saw their grubbiness, their smugness and the hypocrisy of the chapels, only slightly mitigated by the glory of sunshine on bracken on the mountains and the shallow Ogmore River which ran sparkling over the pebbles in spite of the smuts from Wyndham Colliery. They were married in the winter of 1920, Joe being thirty-one years old and May a few years younger. The marriage allayed the doubts of the Goldsworthy family, who were wary of this emancipated woman that Joe had picked up, and they spent a chilly honeymoon at Southerndown on the Ogmore peninsula.

They returned to set up a life together – the first step in those days being to acquire a house. Joe's sister Gwen had married Jim Jones, a colliery winder, and lived in John Street in Ogmore in a terrace close to the river, but Joe preferred to be higher up. "I don't want to live in John Street," he said. "It's too near the river and it's damp." He chose one of a pair of newly-built houses high above the valley in Bryn Road called 2 Vale View Villas. They were set on a rough hillside with a view over the valley to where the trucks were ferried by overhead wires to Lewistown. They bought their house with a mortgage arranged through May's cousin who was a solicitor in Pontypridd. I imagine their combined demobilisation grants helped to pay for the deposit.

The scene was now set for a traditional Welsh marriage: father working in the mine and coming home to bathe in front of the fire, hot water having been scooped from the coal-fired copper in the scullery; mother cleaning and polishing until every vestige of furniture gleamed, then going outside to the yard and beating dirt out of the family washing with a 'dolly' – a pole with a splayed head at the end. One of my earliest memories was watching my mother as she wore a man's cloth cap backwards and sang her favourite hymn while she thumped the dirt out of Joe's blackened clothes at the washtub:

O fryniau Caersalem ceir gweled
(From the hills of Jerusalem you can see)
 Thump, thump.
Holl daith yr anialwch i gyd
(All the journey through the wilderness)
 Thump, thump.
Pryd hyn y daw troeon yr yrfa
(This is where there is a change of course)
 Thump, thump.
Yn felys i lanw ein bryd
(Sweetly filling our mind)
 Thump, thump.
Cawn edrych ar stormydd ac ofnau
(We can look at the storms and the fears)
 Thump, thump.
Ac angau dychrynllyd a'r bedd
(Frightened by death and the grave)
 Thump, thump.

Then triumphantly:

A ninnau ddihangol o'u cyrraedd
(And we escape from their reach)
  Thump, thump.
Yn nofio mewn cariad a hedd
(Swimming in love and peace)
  Thump, THUMP.

May's efforts to emulate the typical Welsh housewife were further enhanced when I was born. There was no way she could have hauled a pram up the twenty steps from Bryn Road to our front door, so she resorted to carrying me around in a shawl as was the custom of most of the women of the valleys. However, neither she nor Joe was really suited to the traditional life and it could be said that they were both play-acting. Joe was already feeling restricted by life underground and was not looking forward to spending the rest of his days as a miner, while May was thinking with nostalgia of the freedom of her time in the Flying Corps. Also, try as she might, she could not shake off the flighty image she seemed to present to the neighbours – the Protheroes and the Joneses – and above all her in-laws in Blackmill.

Joe continued to attend classes at the Workmen's Hall and was becoming more and more absorbed with the history of socialism. When the pre-war rumblings began to get louder, they were accelerated by the insensitivity and greed of the mine owners. Having made a packet during the European conflict they were now suffering from the post-war depression which affected the whole of Western Europe and they tried to re-coup their losses by cutting pay and extending the working week. To a man, the Welsh miners went on strike, their rallying cry being: "NOT A PENNY OFF THE PAY, NOT AN HOUR ON THE DAY."

One by one the pits closed and the ponies were brought up from the dark mines to graze on the blackened grass. But the Union's strike fund was soon exhausted, as was the credit that the local shops were prepared to give, and during the early months of 1921 there was hunger in the valleys. As the days dragged on the housewives began to adopt desperate ruses. They bought condemned black-market meat which was sold cheaply off a lorry at the back of the Workmen's Hall, they boiled up potato peelings with acorns, they scratched in slag-heaps for pieces of coal to light the kitchen fire and they aired the babies' nappies by putting them round their own warm bodies in the freezing houses. In Ogmore there were very few strike breakers even though the owners tried to recruit miners from outside Wales, but some categories were obliged to continue and Gwen's husband Jim Jones belonged to one of them. He was a winder and was responsible for the mechanism which circulated air round the chambers. Once that was stopped the mine would flood and it would be almost impossible to start it up again, so Jim worked and had wages throughout the strike. No doubt Gwen helped her relatives, including my parents, during the bad period.

The months went by and the miners continued to be defiant even though the hoped-for solidarity from the other unions did not materialise. But they couldn't hold out for ever and watch their families starve, so they went back to work having achieved nothing. The sacrifice was made all the more ironic by echoing the earlier one when the country had thrown itself into a war which had nothing to show for it at the end. There was much bitterness in the mines and this fuelled the anti-capitalist fervour which swept through the valleys. Aneurin Bevan was now twenty-four years old and preaching mayhem, standing on a rock (now immortalised) above Tredegar before a crowd of angry men and women. But they didn't turn to revolution, nor even to Communism, probably because that other 'ism' – the vein of Nonconformism – was still very strong at that time. Instead they turned to the Labour Party and from 1921 onwards Ogmore and the rest of Glamorgan regularly returned Labour candidates to Parliament.

I was born in August 1921 while the strike was still on and I think we were better off than most, owing to help from Auntie Gwen and some of my mother's connections, and indeed my impressions of the subsequent two or three years were quite pleasant. A few vivid memories have bizarrely stuck in my mind ever since, one concerning a lost doll. We lived on the side of a mountain not far from an old quarry and I remember tagging along behind a group of children to explore it clutching my only doll, a basic wooden one rather like the manikins used by artists. Somewhere during the expedition I lost it and even though I went back and covered the ground with my mother, it was never found. "Never mind *cariad*," said my mother. "We'll try and get another one." (But we never did!)

The other memory was provoked when my father threatened to drown a stray kitten in the sea. The sea? What was it like? I had never seen the sea but I imagined that it must be like two skies joined together. This was convincingly confirmed when we went on a trip to Porthcawl that summer.

I may have happy memories of those times, but the strike

and its aftermath had left Joe as embittered as his colleagues. To this was added the memory of the price paid by his dead brother, and Joe felt that there would always be blood on the coal as long as one miner was left working in a pit. He determined to get out while he could and to this end he was lucky, because his specialisation as a farrier gave him more opportunities than the average collier. Together with his buttie (fellow farrier) Bill Preece, they agreed that Wales had nothing to offer their young families and decided to cross by train through the new Severn Tunnel to the first major city in England.

Gloucester lies in the Severn Valley on the eastern bank of the river. It is sheltered by the surrounding Cotswold Hills; their soft breezes are very different from the bracing air of the Welsh mountains. ("*Duw*," said Joe, "it's like breathing under a blanket!") The town was first colonised by the Romans – indeed there are relics underneath the pavement in Eastgate Street. They used it as a convenient point for the Legions to cross over the river and quell the barbarians on the other side. Much later a medieval cathedral was built, incorporating a beautiful fan vaulting in the cloister, and it is also the site of one of the repressive Star Chambers which were set up by the Tudors to try recalcitrant citizens. Over the years the Cathedral became the final resting place of various notables including Robert, Duke of Normandy, the son of William the Conqueror. There is a life-sized effigy of him on top of his tomb, complete with armour and spurs. At the time of Joe and Bert Preece's adventure, those spurs came to have an unhappy bearing on the attitude of the local residents to 'those people' who had come from the 'wrong' side of the river.

Chapel-dominated Wales was 'dry' on Sundays, but in

England the pubs were open all day. Youngsters from Wales took advantage of this fact and used to come in bus-loads to drink the beer which the chapel culture at home denied them. Inevitably they got drunk and misbehaved. One Sunday the 'boyo's' lurched into the nave of Gloucester Cathedral and stole one of Robert Duke of Normandy's spurs. This was too much for the straight-laced citizens: drunkenness topped with blasphemy! Wales and all the Welsh were now 'beyond the Pale', so that when Joe and Bert stepped off the train at Gloucester Central they emerged into hostile territory.

CHAPTER 5

An Earlier Adventure

I T IS INTERESTING to reflect that in striking out from the valleys to make a new life in England, Joe and his mate Bert probably thought that they were very daring, but in fact there had been a Cornishman long before who had been equally adventurous. His name was Martin Goldsworthy and he was born in Redruth to Thomas and Elizabeth Goldsworthy (nee Caravasso). She was of Brazilian descent, her ancestors having made the journey to Cornwall when the tin mines were flourishing. Martin was one of seven brothers and sisters and had followed his father's trade of tin miner.

In due course, Martin married a Cornish girl called Mary Kneebone and they produced a daughter, Mary Ann. But then a new life unexpectedly opened up for them, far from Cornwall. The Brazilian authorities were looking for miners to cut a path through the high Sierras to help them establish a brand new capital and Martin, aware of his mother's connections, decided to take up the offer and emigrate. Mary Ann was too young to make the journey, which entailed several weeks at sea by packet steamer, so she was left behind with her grandparents.

Martin and his wife set off in 1850 and soon began to settle down in their new country. Martin did well in his job and we can assume that he helped towards the birth of the new capital, unsurprisingly called Brasilia. The couple had two more children – both boys – who went to the local school and spoke fluent Portuguese. But in 1860 Martin unaccountably died and Mary was left alone, a widow with two young sons. She decided to return to Cornwall to the people she knew, including of course her daughter Mary Ann. There must have been a remarkable reunion when the little party stepped ashore at Plymouth Harbour and the boys met their elder sister. The widow was still young and she was courted by a local stone mason; within a year they were married.

The elder of Mary's two boys, William Henry, followed his new step-father in the stone-mason's craft and was looking forward to constructing more tin mines, but unfortunately by the time he finished his apprenticeship the employment situation in Cornwall had changed drastically. Cornish tin was no longer of commercial value and no new mines were being built, so William Henry's expertise in erecting the stone engine sheds and tall boiler houses was no longer in demand.

However, in contrast to the demise of the Cornish tin industry, the Welsh coal industry was booming. Public transport had to be updated to facilitate the conveyance of coal trucks from the mining valleys to the ports and cities, roads needed to be widened, canals dug and new railway tracks laid down. Since Wales is a country of mountains and ravines, the roads and the canals were built to follow the natural contours, but railways needed a more direct approach with fewer ups and downs. The solution was to span the valleys with viaducts made of stone arches often a hundred feet high. These arches needed stone-masons, so the Great Western Railway recruited men from the dying Cornish tin industry to build them. So one day, William Henry was sent to a small Welsh village called Blackmill.

At first he must have felt pretty isolated. Cornish, or Kernow as it was known, was already dying and William Henry only spoke English (having forgotten most of his Portuguese), whereas most of the locals still spoke Welsh. However, he must have managed to communicate somehow because he was soon courting his landlord's daughter, Gwenllian Lewis. He was quite a catch in that small community, being young and exotically foreign, and he married her in the Paran Chapel by the shallow River Ogwr. Thus began my family's Welsh–Cornish line.

Following the Victorian trend (more due to poverty and the lack of contraceptives than male virility), the couple had eight children including my father and the misbegotten William. It was as a member of this line that Joseph went to England with Bert Preece to stake their claim in a largely hostile country.

CHAPTER 6

Feeling Their Way

WE ARE NOW in the year 1924 and Joe and his buttie are in the middle of their adventure. As with all minorities, the Welsh exiles in England had set up a support network and in the case of Joe and his mate their contact was the Ingram family in Gloucester. Mr Ingram worked shifts for the Great Western Railway which often took him away from home (known as 'double homing'). Mrs Ingram was a tiny woman rather like Grandma Goldsworthy but instead of eight children she only had one, so she had room to put up lodgers.

The Ingrams lived in a small terraced house on the edge of the town with two bedrooms, a kitchen, a parlour and an outside loo. I'm not sure how the extra men managed to fit in, but the house was immaculate with polished furniture and gleaming china – even the outside loo was scrubbed until the wood became soft and spongy. Joe and Bert lived there while they searched for an opening which would allow them to bring their families to join them. It was a daunting process but memories of the 1921 strike and its miseries spurred them on. Both of them were blacksmiths and farriers and this was the age of the horse, so they kept their nerve as they looked for some way of setting up in their trade.

Bert was the first to strike lucky. He found an abandoned forge in a small Gloucestershire village called Longhope and subsequently settled his family there, shoeing the local farm horses. Joe was more drawn to town life and by careful manoeuvring was able to rent a place in the yard of the Black Dog pub in Northgate St. The pub lay parallel to the raised tracks of the Great Western Railway which were supported by arches, some of which were in the pub's yard. Joe set up a forge in one of these arches and gradually built up a thriving business shoeing a variety of horses, from small working nags to the great Shires belonging to the breweries and the railways. Just as Bert had done, he sent for the family to join him.

When I was three years old we left Wales and somehow squashed in with the Ingrams. I was sorry to leave the house above Ogmore; I had got used to the view across the valley where the coal drams slid on wires to the depot at Lewistown and I loved playing in the long narrow garden which followed the slope of the mountain. (My father used to complain about this slope, saying, "It's impossible to grow decent potatoes, the water just drains away.") But of course there was the excitement of going to a new country – what would it be like? Would the people speak English or Welsh? Were there coal mines there? Could I take my cat?

We had been packing our belongings for weeks before the move: the blue patterned dinner-set that Uncle Dai had given my parents as a wedding present, the pots and pans blackened from the coal-fire range, the cutlery, the rugs made from sheep's wool, the pictures (particularly May's framed proficiency certificate from Cardiff) and the poker with the brass handle that Joe had made as a reminder of his last days at the colliery. All these were carefully stacked into an open truck at Ogmore station and taken by rail to Bridgend where they were attached to the steam train which would take us all to Gloucester via the Severn Tunnel.

Joe also took his socialism with him but it was now under

wraps. The previous months of negotiations with the yard owners had made him realise that it would be unwise for him to flaunt his beliefs openly. Within the family and with trusted friends he was as radical as ever, but to the outside world he was the uncontroversial businessman. When I grew older and looked back on those days I appreciated the sacrifices that he had made for his family. He had chosen to keep quiet on many occasions when he would have liked to have spoken, because he found that the persona of 'good old Joe' – rather than the budding socialist – fitted in better with the English people he was obliged to deal with. He gradually became less aggressively Welsh, even giving up a male voice choir he had joined as soon as he arrived (most of the members using tonic sol-fa for their sight-reading). He rarely spoke the old language apart from a quick "*Cau'r drws*" if I left a door open. I suppose one could criticise his attitude but to condemn it would be to ignore the virulent anti-Welsh feeling of those days. Did I want a father or a martyr? Did I want a good life or penury? Of course nobody asked me, but if they had done so I would have unhesitatingly opted for what I got.

I wonder how my father felt as he came to terms with living in England? Embittered by the 1921 strike which had put an end to the cosy family scene that he and May had carefully constructed together, he was now forced to enter into a sort of charade in order to preserve that very family. But maybe I am wrong in this interpretation, maybe those ideas of socialism were not so all-consuming after all. Apart from sticking up for Mahatma Gandhi when the press were putting him down as a 'skinny fanatic in a loincloth', I rarely heard him discuss politics. But I have a treasured photograph taken by the local evening paper, *The Citizen*, of a crowd outside the town hall in Eastgate Street when the results of the 1945 election were announced. Labour had won overwhelmingly and my father was in that crowd. When he came home he said, "I have waited all my life for this."

And what of Violet May during those early years in Gloucester? She had tried to fit into the role of a Welsh housewife but the brutality of the 1921 strike had smashed any idea of normality. What happened to the intrepid WWI volunteer? Where were the skills she had learnt at the commercial college? The answer is that Joe and Bert hadn't made their dangerous gamble on their own, they had been urged on by my mother who had looked around the sad valley and realised that they should get out. Her father had died, her sister had married a charming but feckless Irishman and lived in poverty in Walters Road by Joe's damp river, her other sister Millie had moved to Birmingham with her husband and got hooked on to a fundamentalist religion, while brother Tom was trying to set up a repair shop for the new-fangled phenomenon called wireless. Although she wished him well she realised that he was unlikely to thrive in impoverished Ogmore, and when she thought back to the larks in Blandford Camp – the camaraderie and the expectation that life would be sweeter after the war – she must have said to Joe: "There's no future here. Let's go and see if we can make it in England."

They had no money, only the house – which was still not paid for. Joe wanted to sell it for what they could get but May insisted that they keep it and rent it out to cover the monthly payments (her inherent business sense coming to the fore). This wise decision would stand them in good stead when they took on their next gamble several years later.

CHAPTER 7

Gloucester

W E ARRIVED IN Gloucester and squeezed into the Ingram's tiny house which was situated near Coney Hill Mental Hospital. Mr Ingram had long side-whiskers like Mr Gladstone, and the GWR only gave him a few nights a week at home. Mrs Ingram was everything my mother had tried to be: neat, economical, organised; and the house shone like a new pin. The Ingrams came from mid-Wales and their parents had been hill farmers, so although they had been spared the despoliation of the mining valleys they hadn't been spared rural poverty, and when Mr Ingram was offered a transfer to England he accepted. Their youngest son was a lolloping sixteen-year-old who went to the local technical college. He ignored our family and had a passion for pickles – I saw him one day sneaking into the larder when no-one was looking, to snaffle his favourite food. He was very large and Mrs Ingram was very small, and although I knew nothing about sex or bodies I was puzzled by the fact that he was her son.

Of course we couldn't impose on their kindness for ever, so we moved into the first of a series of rented properties and I began to experience an interesting array of schools. I never knew whether the frequent moves were due to my parents being too fussy or if they were shielding me from any discrimination that may have occurred due to their Welshness.

The list of properties was impressive: two rooms in Dean's Walk (Gloucester, being a cathedral city, had many street names with religious connotations); a couple of rooms over a shoe shop in Kingsholme Road; a basement in Brunswick Square; a house on the edge of the city called 'Louvain' (after a WWI battle about which Joe laconically stated, "I was in that,") and finally, a whole house with a shop attached in St Aldate Street near the cattle market, which in those days was in the centre of the town.

Whenever we found a place incorporating a shop, my mother took over the running of it and the money she earned helped Joe as he struggled to build up his business. It was while helping in the shoe shop in Kingsholme Road that she came across a type of commercialism that she hadn't been taught in her Cardiff College. The owner adopted many ruses to sell his shoes. If a customer tried on a pair of shoes which didn't fit over her bunions, the owner would say, "Don't worry, I will get a bigger size from the manufacturer." In effect he would wet and stretch the leather in his back room and present the same shoes to her when she next called – and charge her for postage!

My first school was Mount Street Junior; to get there I walked hurriedly along the Cathedral lanes with old tombs set in the walls. Next there was a small church school in Brunswick Square where we had a talk from the vicar every Wednesday morning. When we were living in the house called 'Louvain' I went to Tredworth School where my route went past the main town cemetery. I was convinced that the white tombstones were for the good people and the weathered black ones for the bad, and I ran past that place as quickly as I could. My last school before the 11 plus exam was out of our catchment area (a bus ride away), but my mother wangled a place for me because it had a good reputation. It was there that I blossomed and passed the exam to go to the local grammar school. Whether I got through academically or if it was due to the fixed smile I made sure I had a on my face when I attended the interview with my mother, I will never know. In all, I went to four junior schools in five years and I don't think it did me any harm, in spite of what modern educationalists might say.

I encountered very little flak for being Welsh, or maybe I was too naive to notice. I only remember one incident in junior school when I read aloud in class: "Last Saturday I went with my mother to the cop." In Wales we abbreviated the Co-operative Society to 'cop' instead of the English 'co-op', and my classmates laughed at the unfamiliar sound.

"That's enough," said the teacher. "Carry on, Eva."

By the time I went to secondary school my intonations had flattened and I did not seem so obviously Welsh.

Whereas Joe had tried to bring his socialism to Gloucester without success, May brought her Methodism – a more acceptable 'ism'. She happily attended the nearest chapel and joined in with the social gatherings. At one stage she was even invited by a Lydney pastor to give a talk at their annual Ladies' Day event. Lydney is a small town in the Forest of Dean which serves as a demarcation between England and Wales. The people of the forest had their own particular dialect and jealously preserved their ancient rights to mine the surface coal of the area. It took some courage to address a meeting in front of such independent people and I treasure a poster that was circulated at the time announcing 'A Talk by Mrs Goldsworthy of Gloucester'.

Meanwhile, Joe and Bert were building up their shoeing business from scratch. At that time Gloucester was full of horses. As well as the great Shire horses of the GWR and the breweries with their jingling harnesses and feet as big as dinner plates, there were smaller breeds delivering anything that needed to be conveyed from A to B: milk, bread, furniture, parcels and the ubiquitous rag-and-bone man. My father shod them all, just as he had shod those trembling creatures in France after a battle. Although he refused to talk about the hand-to-hand trench warfare, he sometimes told me anecdotes about the horses. "The police horses were fine in battle," he said. "Rock-solid. But the thoroughbreds that some of the officers brought with them suffered a lot. I suppose it was shellshock, but in those days the condition wasn't understood, either for men or horses."

I used to love visiting him in his forge under the arches. The cavernous ceiling shook with each passing train, the walls were lined with implements of his trade – wrenches, hammers, rasps and tongs, like medieval instruments of torture – and in one corner was the flat glowing fire with its enormous bellows. In pride of place in front of the fire was the anvil he had managed to spirit out of the mine in Nant-y-moel which had helped him shape horse-shoes for his beloved pit ponies.

I was very proud of my father with his leather apron and gnarled workman's hands, and I loved to hear the clip-clop of the magnificent Shires as they came down the cobbled yard to be shod, their harnesses reflecting the slanting sunshine. But then came the scary part when my father grasped one of those great feet against his apron (having first prised off the old shoe), then lifted the new shoe off the fire with large tongs and pressed it on to the dead horn of the horse's hoof. The acrid smell as the shoe bedded in and the way the horse tried to jerk away from my father's vice-like grip was a 'moment of truth' that I would never forget. It was dark under that railway arch but light came in from the yard. I often used to wonder what the same operation must have been like in the pitch-black mine when he shod the pit ponies.

Many years later when I was teaching mathematics in London, I used to pass the Hyde Park Barracks in Kensington on my way to school. This impressive building is the home of the Household Cavalry, being only three-quarters of a mile from Buckingham Palace. As befits a cavalry regiment it houses a working forge, so that each morning as I passed by I heard the familiar sound of hammer on anvil and smelled the stench of burning horn. As I continued on my way up to Holland Park Comprehensive I was touched with a sense of nostalgia.

CHAPTER 8

The General Strike

ALTHOUGH JOE HAD got out, the unrest provoked by the miners' strike of 1921 had not gone away. Conditions for the English miners in Durham and Clydeside were as bad as in Wales. To this was added the dissatisfaction of the whole of the working class up and down the country. Our regular newspaper was the *Daily Herald*, founded by the radical politician George Lansbury but taken over by the TUC. My father read it assiduously every morning. "It's the only paper that tells the truth," he said, but rather shamefacedly kept it out of sight in a drawer in the dresser.

Although the *Daily Herald* was far from subversive, it certainly countered the scare stories of the other tabloids which saw 'reds under the beds' when even the mildest socialist views were mooted. It must be said that by now the Communists were trying hard to infiltrate the Welsh Valleys (Maerdy in the Rhondda was known as 'little Moscow'), but for the most part the working class, including the miners, just wanted better pay and conditions and had no taste for insurgency. It was only when no improvements were forthcoming and when a temporary subsidy which had been given to the miners as a palliative came to an end, that the TUC authorised a general strike.

It began at midnight on 1 May 1926 and the response was absolute. Even the print workers came out so there were no newspapers, but in a subsequent editorial the *Daily Herald* described that first morning – the eerie silence, no trains, no buses on the streets, no whistling building workers, no rattle of the letterboxes... I wonder if it reminded the older war veterans of a similar eerie silence which fell over the battlefields when the guns stopped eight years previously. Maybe they hoped that this time there would not be a betrayal of the working class.

During the strike the country stumbled on with the help of well-meaning amateurs who drove trains and buses and helped unload perishable food supplies, usually with a police escort to protect them from striking pickets. Many of the volunteers were undergraduates or public schoolboys enjoying the 'lark' and this exacerbated the enmity between the working class and the 'toffs'. On 12 May, after prolonged discussions between the TUC and the politicians, the strike was called off. It had lasted eleven days and the workers returned to their jobs having achieved almost nothing. The general opinion was that of betrayal and the TUC took many years to recapture the confidence of the working man. The South Wales miners, however, refused to accept the TUC agenda and as in 1921, stayed out a further six months until December 1926 when starvation again defeated them and they went back to work on marginally worse terms.

In Gloucester, Joe took no part in the strike. If he had been in Wales he would undoubtedly have been part of the militancy, whereas in England he was just an observer and the guardian of his family. He and Bert were of course self-employed, and the horses still needed to be shod.

After the General Strike, life in Gloucester reverted to normal; not so the other side of the Severn. Perhaps the hopes of the English had not been as high as in Wales, where the rhetoric of the preachers in the chapels and the socialists up on the mountains had been very persuasive, so that when the promised kingdom did not materialise the disappointment was all the greater.

We always went 'home' for Christmas and 1926 was no exception. We set off on a second-hand motorbike and sidecar (my mother and I in the sidecar) with the luggage and presents strapped to the pillion seat. All went well until we got to Abergavenny in Monmouthshire where we broke down. Abergavenny is a small farming town surrounded by hills, the highest of which is called the 'Sugar Loaf' because of its conical shape. As I looked up at it I wondered what sort of a Christmas we would have. "Don't worry," said my mother briskly. She picked up the lightest of the luggage and we walked to the station, leaving Joe to get the bike fixed. Happily there was a train going to Bridgend and moreover it was due to meet a connection going to Ogmore. Some hours later we arrived tired and hungry at Auntie Gwen's house in John Street and found Joe already there drinking tea, having had the bike repaired sooner than expected!

They did their best to give me a good Christmas and Auntie Gwen bustled about and hastily put together a stocking with an apple at the bottom, but even I felt the drag of defeat and the obvious signs of poverty. I remember boarded-up shops and thin, grey-faced men hanging around on street corners. The coal mine owners had taken their revenge and there had been savage cuts in employment, most of all for the so-called 'agitators'. The burning aim of most of the youngsters in Ogmore was to get out. "Two strikes on one lifetime is two too many," said Auntie Gwen. The despair in the valleys was getting her down, even though Jim Jones had been able to keep working through both stoppages because of his vital work as a winder.

Someone who had succeeded in breaking loose was Gwen's eldest son Reginald. After he left school he had worked in the outfitting department of the Gwalia, but in his late teens had gone to London to seek his fortune and was fortunate to get a job in the same line in Austin Reed. He was a fine upstanding lad who looked older than his years, and after a time he really struck lucky and teamed up with a master tailor called Chamberlain. Together they began their own retail clothing business and it prospered. Years later when I had grown up and was living in London I bought a camel hair coat from one of their branches in Regent Street.

Reginald had grown to be a big, shambling man with unlimited confidence. As he grew more successful he may have felt that having parents who lived in a decaying Welsh valley did not fit in with his image, so he generously decided to set them up in England, buying them a semi-detached house in Sutton, Surrey and arranging for his father to take over a window-cleaning business. Auntie Gwen adapted well to the drastic change in their lifestyle but Uncle Jim was a typical innocent abroad. I was told that when a female client paid him for cleaning her windows and he saw her scarlet painted finger nails he felt obliged to say, "Excuse me, madam, but I think you are bleeding." Jim never got used to English urban life and yearned for the valleys he had left behind. Once on their way back to Ogmore for a funeral they stayed with us at St Aldate Street. When Jim got up in the morning and heard the animals in the nearby cattle market, he said with fervour, "Thank God for the sound of a sheep."

My parents were an interesting couple. Joe was the handsome one, as a photograph I still have of him demonstrates. May had a sharp intelligent face which just missed being beautiful, but she used her elongated features to play her favourite party trick of touching the end of her nose with the tip of her tongue. Joe had the charm and May had the cunning and between them they carved out a life for themselves in a largely unsympathetic town. The ties with Wales were still strong and we tried to get back 'home' as often as possible but I began to notice that we were gradually visiting the Principality less frequently – we even missed out one Christmas entirely! Perhaps the dreariness of the valleys was beginning to get us down; perhaps my father felt a sense of guilt that he had deserted his friends and family back home. Whatever the reason, the motor-bike and sidecar rarely made the trip again to *gwlad Cymru*.

An added disincentive as far as May was concerned was that the Edwards family in Walters Road had begun to disintegrate. Her sister Millie had already left home and later married an Englishman called Charlie who was a devout Christadelphian; they went to live in an area of Birmingham called 'Happy Valley'. Sister Ivy had married an Irishman called Pat Doyle but she caught typhoid fever and died in Ogmore fever hospital. Brother Tom was diagnosed with cancer and married his nurse Eunice but died after the disease spread through his body, even though he was flown from Cardiff to Bristol hospital for treatment thus avoiding the long journey round the estuary. The only family members left in Ogmore were Tom's wife and Ivy's husband. Tom had treated Pat very badly and called him an "Irish wimp," when he failed to start up a car by swinging the front starter-handle. My auntie Ivy had been the creative one in the family and I used to love visiting the house in Walters Road which she had decorated with Chinese wallpaper and hanging mobiles. They were still there after she died.

CHAPTER 9

Barton Fair

A LTHOUGH THE GLOUCESTER branch of the family went to Wales less frequently, one element of the Goldsworthy clan visited us. My cousin William had been working for his brother David's coal delivery business, then took over and expanded it when David died. From then on he was always referred to as 'Bill Coal'. He did sufficiently well to pay a yearly visit to Gloucester with his wife Martha and their children in order to go to Barton Fair, which took place every autumn on the boggy meadow at the bottom of Westgate Street.

The meadow was the winter home of the itinerant gypsies and showmen who operated throughout the 'Four Shires'. My first school, Mount Street, was on a rise just above it and this is where I learnt that in the pecking order of those times, we – the people from the wrong side of the Severn – were not on the very bottom rung of the ladder. That place was occupied by the gypsies, or 'diddycois' as they were known locally. Their children came to my infant school and I am afraid that I joined in with the disdain with which they were treated. They were ragged and smelly and spoke with a strange accent, so perhaps my small self could be forgiven, though not excused, for my attitude.

Barton Fair was the high point of the town's schedule and attracted people from miles around. There were several families which were dominant in the fairground world, among them the Edwards (no relation) and the Cotterals who controlled most of the stalls and the booths and amusements. The fair came hard on the heels of the big autumn cattle market which used to take place in November. Just as the farmers from Lydney, Huntley, Redmarley and as far a-field as Hereford and Evesham came to the market to sell their cattle or buy new stock, so they were inveigled by their wives and children to take them to the fair.

There were dodgems, swings, a helter-skelter, roll-penny stalls, coconut shies, tombolas, gypsy fortune tellers, and of course the giant round-a-bout with stately horses moving up and down on shiny poles accompanied by an electric organ which played loud enough to be heard as far away as the cloisters of the Cathedral. My friends and I used to tramp through the November mud which was churned up by hundreds of feet, eating candy floss and toffee apples and wasting our carefully hoarded pennies on all sorts of nonsense. After all, what was money for but to throw it away at Barton Fair?

Auntie Martha and my mother would go straight to the china auction which was set up in a prominent part of the meadow on a high platform. The auctioneer echoed his counterpart in the cattle market earlier in the week, but he was wittier and more persuasive and played on the credulity of his audience. It was a Dutch auction in which an item was introduced at a high price and then the auctioneer would reduce it gradually until a bid was made. The tension was enormous because if you bid too soon you might lose a bargain, yet if you waited too long you would lose the opportunity. Throughout the proceedings the auctioneer would crack jokes, make indiscreet suggestions, urge on the punters (who were mostly women) and extol the virtues of whatever gimcrack item he was holding up. But not all the china was rubbish and many people, including my auntie Martha, went away satisfied.

Unhappily, the Welsh valleys continued to moulder and Joe must have thought many times how lucky he was to have left when he did, otherwise he might have been one of the grey ghosts in the grey towns. The people of the cathedral city (known as 'Gloucester Spots' after the local breed of pig) did not escape a certain amount of belt-tightening, but on the whole they managed to lead a passable life. As the general conditions gradually improved, so did life for May and Joe. May was absorbed in looking after the shop in St Aldate Street and sorting out both Joe and Bert's paperwork, while Joe continued to shoe horses under the arches in the Black Dog yard. In the evenings he drank with like-minded mates who solved the evils of the world, always stopping short of the 'S' word. We even acquired a second-hand motor car as a replacement for the motor bike; it was a Morris Oxford Coupe with celluloid windows which remained in place even when the hood was drawn back, so that my view of the countryside was always tinged with yellow.

But this easy life was not to last, partly because of the advent of the motor car. Joe had built up a successful business with clientele from the GWR, the breweries and other tradesmen, but with the coming of the combustion engine horses weren't needed anymore. In Longhope, Bert didn't feel the draught because he had already switched to catering for the hunting and gymkhana crowd, but Joe's socialism, dormant though it was, didn't take kindly to the thought of touting for work from the local 'Hooray Henrys' and 'Thelwell Misses'. As the income from the smithy became less and less, my parents set up a council of war, instigated of course by my mother, to discuss the possibility of a change of tack.

CHAPTER 10

Smith & Sons (1)

THERE WAS ANOTHER railway arch next to Joe's forge and it was occupied by a firm which specialised in making, hiring and repairing large marquees. I had seen its logo stamped on odd bits of canvas that had come our way: 'SMITH & SONS Tenting Manufacturers'. The proprietor had recently died and the business was up for sale. Should Joe switch to this new occupation which had nothing to do with the skills for which he had been trained? He was now well into his forties and most men at that stage would have hoped to settle down quietly in the same job until they died (life-expectancy for the working class in those days was around sixty).

"It is an opportunity," said May.

"I'm not sure if I've got the nerve," Joe replied.

"You're the bravest man I know."

"We haven't any money."

"We've got the house at Ogmore."

Largely owing to my mother's insistence they sold Vale View Villas and bought the tenting business. With it came a house and a shop in Worcester Street, a working lorry, and Mr Fudge who had been with the previous owner as a machinist, making tents.

So we moved again, this time to Worcester Street which was halfway between the Black Dog yard and the Cathedral.

My father only needed to cross the road to go to work and I could lie in bed and listen to the Cathedral bells tolling every hour. On the down side there was the stench from the tallow factory in Westgate Street when the wind was blowing in the wrong direction.

Joe was now an employer for the first time in his life and to begin with the whole thing went very badly. Mr Fudge had been running the business when the old man was ill and he resented the newcomer who had taken it on. There was also a clash of personalities between the Englishman who had imbibed prejudice at his mother's knee and the Welshman who, to be frank, had a very short fuse. I remember Joe grumbling to May about the problem and explaining that although he found it impossible to work with the man he couldn't do without him. Somehow it got resolved; Mr Fudge moved to another tenting firm in Worcester and Smith & Sons stopped making their own tents and concentrated instead on the hiring part of the business.

When I was fourteen years old, my sister Sheila was born. I had no warning of the event, so when the ambulance came one night and took my mother away to hospital I was convinced that she was going to die. I couldn't get back to sleep since I was expecting the worst, but when Mrs Perkins the next-door neighbour came the following morning and told me in unctuous terms that I had a little sister, I was furious. Why hadn't they told me? I knew all about babies, the biology teacher at the high school had told us how the male toad's big thumb helped the female toad to make them. Everyone must have known about the pregnancy except me, including Mrs Perkins who wasn't even a member of the family!

The resentment smouldered for years, right up to the present day when my middle daughter Penny casually dropped the information that Granny had told her that she hadn't known she was pregnant until the seventh month, when she went to the doctor complaining of indigestion. We were all very ignorant in those days and to talk about pregnancy was considered 'talking dirty'. My father on the other hand was more robust in his attitude and I often heard him refer to a pregnancy as "a portmanteau job". The general reticence about referring to sex, coupled with my mother's tendency to malapropism (viz. Sheridan's play *The Rivals*), sometimes led to bizarre situations. For example, she could never bring herself to say 'sex' and elided it into 'sec' which took away the nastier implications.

Sheila also told me of an incident which happened when as a child she was sent to the chemist with a note. The chemist read it unbelievingly.

"Is this the amount you want?" he asked.

"Yes," said my trusting sister.

"Well," said the chemist, "with this lot you could blow up Northgate Street."

May had asked for TNT, an explosive, instead of DDT, an insecticide.

As well as the fourteen-year gap between my sister and myself, we were different in appearance. I had the good looks which eventually lured me to the stage whereas Sheila grew up to be the gamin type with cropped hair and was good at games. She was loved even though she hadn't been expected, but the family now faced a quandary. Could May manage to look after a new baby, serve in the shop and do the paperwork? The situation was solved by the recruitment of a series of young women who were employed to live in as home-help and baby-minder. To begin with they were recruited through my parents' connections in Wales.

The first one was Gwennie Nott. She was a child of the valleys, wide eyed and solemn, awed by the sight of her first big town. She came provided with woolly vests and sensible shoes, and was inculcated with the lore of the *gwraig tŷ* (housewife) to the extent that the pots and pans and furniture gleamed as brilliantly as I remembered them from our stay at the Ingrams. But Gwennie was too young and she became homesick for her family in the valleys, so after a few months she left. The next one was Iris, again from the valleys but older and more worldly-wise. She seemed fine to me and told me wonderful bed-time stories (May's war-time reminiscences having long since petered out), but she and my mother didn't get on well together over various matters which I didn't understand, so she also left. Finally there was Phyllis, who revolutionised the lives of Sheila and myself. She wasn't from Wales but the Forest of Dean, that hinterland behind the Severn which straddles Wales and England, where my mother had once given a talk on Methodism. Moreover, it was near enough to Gloucester for Phyllis to go home to her family for the odd weekend.

My dear mother would never have considered herself a professional housewife – and it showed! Cleaning, polishing and cooking didn't come naturally to her, but Phyllis soon became our surrogate mother. She instigated regular bath nights and tooth cleanings, she took my sister for daily walks in the pram and we had 'afters' all through the week instead of just with the Sunday roast. My favourite was 'Railway Pudding', a sponge with a thick layer of raspberry jam. Phyllis stayed with us for several years until she got married. She was a short, stubby woman with blunt features and false teeth, but I remember her as one of the more positive elements in my childhood.

CHAPTER 11

Teenage Angst

I WAS GRADUALLY growing up and came under a variety of influences between the years of eleven and sixteen, the dominant ones being the cinema, my secondary school and the public library in Brunswick Road.

The cinema, the Theatre de Lux, was just round the corner from our shop – in fact the back entrance led out on to Worcester Street. As it was so near, my mother, who was tied to looking after the shop, allowed me to go alone on Saturday afternoons and I saw a different film each week. The building was in the prevalent style of the 1930s – angular with splashes of bright colour outside and luxurious seats upholstered in maroon plush inside. To my everlasting shame I was once so engrossed in a particularly thrilling film that I wee-ed on the maroon plush rather than break the spell and go to the ladies.

One of my most vivid memories is of a film called *The Volga Boatman*. It showed Russian peasants, men and women, pulling heavy barges along the river, urged on by a task-master with whips. Then, after a lot of fighting in front of the Winter Palace, the subsequent scene showed a different set of men and women pulling those same barges with a peasant cracking the whip instead. I remember seeing the women's silk dresses dragging through the mud and the men's high leather boots, by now down-at-heel with wear and splitting open. There was the inevitable love scene between a Russian aristocrat and a peasant, with the woman declaiming, "By my Volga boatman's side I will stand!"

Another memory is of a film about an institution where a woman was scrubbing a floor but hesitated in putting her hands into the very hot water, so the presiding matron forcefully pushed them into the steaming bucket. Did I even then empathize with the underdog? Was Joe's socialism stirring in me also?

My secondary school was the local grammar in Denmark Road. It was a brisk half-hour walk from Worcester Street and I did the journey twice a day, it being near enough for me to go home for lunch. It was an imposing brick building with a shrubbery at the entrance and a playing field behind, but the aspect which most impressed me as a twelve-year-old in new uniform and stiff brimmed hat, was the parquet flooring in the hall. To my eyes it was vast and awe inspiring.

There were natural divisions between the posh girls who came from the countryside, stayed to lunch and whose parents paid their fees – Gwen Hudson and Rene A'bear, for example – and the 'scholarship girls' like me who were from the city. The posh ones wore cardigans which were hand knitted by their mothers in the school colours and were different from the regulation ones us mortals wore. They came to school in cars and developed catchphrases which we didn't understand. As we got older they also had the nerve to flirt with the boys from Sir Thomas Riche's school, whose playing field was just down the road.

The covert class system didn't worry me; in fact I may have even contributed to it when Helen arrived in the middle of the third term of our first year. She was lumpy and unprepossessing with owl-like glasses, but she was very bright academically. However, this didn't help her to integrate with us and she didn't seem to fit into any of our groups. She had a good singing voice and I remember her singing a Schubert song and pronouncing the German words very accurately, but her very abilities seemed to alienate her and she remained friendless. Many years later when I looked back on those days I realised that she was a Jew. How I wish that I had had the courage to champion her!

The joy of my school life was the arrival of the new English teacher, Miss Noreen Neve. She took us for Shakespeare and we immediately began to act instead of simply reading from the printed page. Marc Anthony declaimed over the dying Caesar who was lying on the parquet floor in the school hall, Lady Macbeth strode back from killing the guards, brandishing a ruler instead of a bloody knife, and I grew to love every minute of our double English periods. The culmination was when I performed on the school stage as Oberon in a presentation of *A Midsummer's Night's Dream*. Our parents were invited but, unhappily, neither of mine came. However, I achieved a certain amount of glory by carrying on my dialogue with Puck when one of the ten-foot-high stage trees fell over in front of us. It wasn't courage, just an unwillingness to let anything come between Shakespeare and me. Indeed, I had become obsessed with the Bard and when I reached the sixth form I was not interested in going to a university, but prevailed upon my parents to let me leave and join a local repertory company. This was not the life that my parents had planned, but I must have been very persistent because in the end they agreed and I went on the stage. However, my life on the boards wasn't too successful and it ended when war came. I went home and, ironically, found myself on fire-watch duty at the very same school I had left.

During those six years at school and before I became so

obsessed with Shakespeare, I used to haunt the Public Library in Brunswick Road and devoured all the books by Angela Brazil. She specialised in girls' boarding school life, with 'larks in the dorm' and so on. Inherent in such stories was the implied home background of the girls, with father being 'something in the city' and mother presiding over a small staff of cook, gardener and housekeeper. I used to fantasise that our sequence of resident maids approximated to this arrangement. Later when I became stage-struck I devoured any books to do with the theatre, principally biographies of Noel Coward and Gertrude Laurence, as well as a dizzying biography of the dancer Nureyev.

CHAPTER 12

Smith & Sons (2)

T HE EMPLOYMENT OF extra help in the house eased the family situation, so May was able to continue working in the shop and Joe could devote himself to his new venture. He had very few regrets in leaving blacksmithing; after all, it was a taxing job only mitigated by his love for horses, and I doubt if he could have carried on much longer because lifting up the feet of those great Shire horses needed a young man's strength. He had only rented the arch under the railway and when he left, the lessees who owned it found difficulty in finding another tenant because no-one wanted to take over from a failing business. So the forge remained idle, the iron instruments rusting on the walls, until a supermarket took the place on as a store room. Next door at Smith & Sons, however, Joe realised that he had stumbled upon a winner.

Gloucestershire had escaped the despoliation of industrial Britain and many families, having profited from the growth of empire and the slave trade, had built large country houses on the county's green fields and hills. But as the source of their wealth began to dry up, they began to find it hard to maintain these opulent white elephants, even though in some instances the family had owned the property for several generations. As a result, many were sold and their contents auctioned. This is where Joe came in, for the valuable pictures and furniture would be set out in a marquee, waiting for the public to come and view them. As one by one the families of the gentry began to feel the pinch, so Smith & Sons, in tandem with the auctioneers Bruton & Knowles, invaded the immaculate front lawns.

Putting up a large tent is no easy matter. First of all the main poles have to be erected, either two or three depending on the size of the marquee. They are thirty feet high with a diameter of around eight inches and need at least three men to manhandle them into an upright position, but before this is done they are slotted through the reinforced holes in the canvas which will eventually form the roof. When the poles are upright, they are steadied and secured to the ground with thick ropes which are held down by large wooden tent pegs. The canvas is then pulled up to the top of each pole, rather like a flag being raised, and the 'roof' is pulled out to form a circle or an oblong. It is secured in place by smaller poles which are kept vertical by the use of guy ropes. Finally, the 'skirt' of the tent is hooked on to the circumference of the roof and the procedure is complete.

Joe needed a team to help him with these operations, so he once again became an employer; but this time he avoided anyone like Mr Fudge. He chose to employ casual labour, men who had no pretensions and shunned regular work but were prepared to have a go if the money was right. He got on well with them – they reminded him of his troops when he was a sergeant in the army: rough, good-hearted, sometimes even deferential! They were polite to May when she paid them at the end of the week and they seemed genuinely fond of 'the gaffer'. They were also sensitive enough to be aware of the poignancy of the situation when a soon-to-be-superannuated servant from the big house brought them a tray of tea. In deference to the setting they tipped their dregs into an empty cup, which Joe unwittingly drank from one day. "Oi!" said one of them. "You're drinking the slops." My father was a very fastidious man and it took him a long time to recover from that incident.

Back in Worcester Street May was now in her element. Although the shop was meant as a mere adjunct to the tenting business, she expanded it and developed a whole new set of customers. Initially it had dealt only in items associated with tent-making, but she introduced other lines which incorporated anything to do with farming – baler twine, string, rabbit nets, ferret collars, china eggs, horse halters and a heavy lump of metal shaped like a sausage.

"What is that for?" I asked.

"It's for a bull," she said, and quickly changed the subject.

The shop didn't look very prepossessing, being on the non-sunny side of the street with a large bay window into which an assortment of items were displayed haphazardly. Prospective customers were usually startled when they walked through the entrance because a large bell balanced above the door gave an almighty clang. In the window, enormous balls of orange binder twine dwarfed the little balls of household string which came in two colours – white for jute, brown for hemp – then higher up a tangle of rabbit nets hung from the ceiling. The diddycois used to buy them by the dozen for their midnight poaching but my mother pretended to be unaware of these activities, even though she may have just sold some binder twine to the very farmer they were about to rob. Winking in the darkness at the back of the shop were strings of brass medallions used by the carters of the GWR and the breweries to decorate their great Shire horses. Then lining one of the walls were tarpaulins of various sizes, stiff with chemicals which made them waterproof. The smell of these chemicals permeated the shop – acrid, tart, but not altogether unpleasant. So strong was the smell that one could almost taste it.

My dainty mother presided over this display with her soft South Wales voice which contrasted sharply with the more robust accents of her customers, who were gypsies, bluff farmers, poachers (one even carried a ferret in his top pocket!) and landed gentry. The contrast may have had something to do with the attraction of her shop which was well known beyond the city limits, even as far as the Forest of Dean. My mother was often referred to as 'the lady of the string shop'.

Encouraged by her success, May now embarked on serving the new camping craze brought about by the sudden post-war awareness of the joys of healthy living. She hired out small tents and sleeping bags to youngsters who wanted a taste of the countryside. Perhaps she became too ambitious and over-reached the capacity of one woman working on her own, because from time to time there were mistakes. For example, a group of campers setting up their tent in a remote part of the Cotswolds found an essential pole missing! But she seems to have been forgiven, perhaps because she was a lone woman in a largely male environment.

The paperwork necessary for running the expanded shop was considerable, so Joe built an office at the back made of plywood. Here the telephone and manual typewriter were installed (this was 1935) and for the first time in her life May was in charge of her own establishment. As well as the shop accounts she still did the books for Bert Preece, and of course Joe's new business entailed more typing and telephoning than when he was a blacksmith. May felt that she was at last fulfilling the promise she had shown all those years ago in Cardiff. Soon both my parents began to feel that their daring move to England and their subsequent (even more daring) move to Worcester Street had been a success.

"Seven number Worcester Street," as my sister called it, was a rambling old place with a fascinating history. It had been a farmhouse in the days before Gloucester City began to encroach on the surrounding fields and meadows. It still had its outhouses and a separate two-storey brick barn. The back way led on to Hare Lane which had once housed many working class families but was now derelict. The council in their wisdom had bulldozed the tenement houses and moved the families into concrete boxes miles from the town centre in a place they euphemistically called 'The White City'. The next stage was to develop the area now freed by the bulldozers, but this failed to attract investors so Hare Lane remained an eyesore for many years.

The council was also involved in what I considered to be an iniquitous planning error involving an alley which led from Westgate Street to the Cathedral. This was made up of small shops on both sides, many of them dating back to the eighteenth century, and at the end there was an archway leading to College Green and the great West Door of the Cathedral. I used to love walking through this alley and looking into the tiny bottle-glass shop windows. It emanated an enclosed, secret air enhanced by the fact that in the evenings it seemed rather dark and sinister. Unhappily, the council gave a branch of Timothy White's pharmaceutical chain permission to build on the right-hand side, and one dreadful morning bulldozers came and pulled down all the little shops to make way for a brand new building. The mystery was shattered; the daylight and the noise of traffic turned the precious little enclave into an open throughway and Gloucester lost a small piece of itself. The site is now only remembered in the following lines of Beatrix Potter:

> In the time of swords and periwigs and full-skirted coats with
> flowered lappets – when gentlemen wore ruffles and gold-
> laced waistcoats lined with paduasoy or taffeta – there lived a
> tailor in Gloucester. He sat in the window of a little shop in
> Westgate Street, cross-legged on a table from morning till dark.
> All day long while the light lasted he sewed and snippetted,
> piecing out his satin, and pompadour, and lutestring; stuffs
> had strange names, and were very expensive in the days of
> the Tailor of Gloucester.

Still on the theme of council misdemeanours, or balls-ups
as my father used to say, I must explain that the previous
owners of our house in Worcester Street had installed
a bathroom and a separate indoor lavatory. But what a
bathroom and what a lavatory! Indoor lavatories had not
really caught on because although no-one liked going outside
to the toilet at inconvenient times, we had got used to using
chamber pots (or guzunders) which tucked under the bed for
the occasional piss, but the thought of doing the 'big one'
inside the house struck most people as unhealthy. Of course
with later improvements in ventilation and architect-designed
bathrooms and toilets the inside loo has been accepted, but
thinking back to Worcester Street in the 1930s the original
objection was valid. Our loo was at the head of the stairs in
a little cubicle with a tiny window allowing insufficient air
circulation and had only more or less adequate plumbing. We
never mentioned it to each other but I remember that there
was a definite 'pong' coming from that indoor lavatory. The
bathroom, on the other hand, wasn't in the least bit unhealthy
– just the reverse. The builders, instead of installing it inside
the house, had tacked it on to an outside wall two storeys up.

It was constructed of slatted wood with a wooden floor and was just long enough to accommodate a bath with one long window above it. I used to think that it was like a tree house, except that a tree house would have been more substantial. During WWII when we crouched in our home-made bomb shelter, I was always surprised when we emerged the next morning to look up and find that the bathroom was still there. One of my many fantasies was to be in the bath when it was blown away and to see Gloucester from an advantageous height.

To be fair, both the bathroom and the lavatory must have been erected before the advent of planning regulations; not so our back entry which gave on to Hare Lane. The council had been prodded into action by an American descendant of one of the Pilgrim Fathers who had gone to America to escape from Catholic persecution. He discovered that his ancestor had lived in the Raven Tavern at the top of Hare Lane and he was anxious to come over and see it. Fortunately, it had escaped the bulldozers but had become derelict. When the council hurriedly began the renovation they found that a part of it encroached on our back way. There were prolonged negotiations with my father, money changed hands, and there is now a blue plaque on the Raven Tavern wall rather like the ones in London which commemorate notable events and people.

Just as May's life had become more fulfilling, so Joe's world expanded and helped him to forget his years as a miner. The stint working as a blacksmith in the Black Dog yard had been an improvement on working underground, but his new life in the tenting business driving around Gloucestershire in the lorry and putting up tents on the lawns of magnificent country houses was even better, opening his eyes to the countryside, the gentry and even royalty! I remember him being particularly taken with the Duchess of Gloucester: "A very nice little woman," he used to say. Above all he had discovered and fallen in love with the Cotswolds. It makes me feel good in retrospect to realise that this man who had breathed methane-tainted air in his youth could now breathe the pure air of Stonehouse, Stroud, Brimscombe and Painswick Beacon. Although Joe had a fine singing voice he was no poet, but there were others who could express his delight for him, such as soldier-poet FW Harvey in his poem *On Painswick Beacon* – from where it is possible to see the shires of Gloucester, Worcester, Hereford, Monmouth and Oxford:

> Here lie counties five in a wagon wheel
> There quick Severn like a silver eel
> Wriggles through the pastures green and pale stubble
> There, sending up its quiet coloured bubble
> Of earth, May Hill floats on a flaming sky
> And, marvelling at all, forgetting trouble
> Here – home again – stand I.

Not wonderful poetry, but to me it is very apposite. FW Harvey served in WWI and the poem describes his return on leave from France. During WWII, I also stood on Painswick Beacon and saw a flaming sky, but it was Bristol burning.

CHAPTER 13

"A life that was disappearing"

A S A FAMILY we all profited from Joe's love of the Cotswolds because as well as house sales he also covered flower shows and horse races – indeed any event which needed a marquee. Every Easter, for example, we would take a day out and go to the point-to-point races above Winchcombe. Joe checked the guy ropes while my mother, young sister and I watched the 'County' jumping over hurdles. Joe, passionate as he was about horses, offered to have me taught to ride. I would have enjoyed learning but a certain perversity which has always dogged me made me refuse. I am sure Joe was disappointed because at rock bottom he yearned for a son, and I sometimes found myself an unwilling substitute. This was sometimes to my advantage, sometimes not; I have memories of him taking me to suffer long boring afternoons at the Wagon Works grounds in Gloucester to watch the cricket. Joe's tents were there and he went around checking the tightness of the guy ropes while I sat in a privileged seat in the stands looking at this incomprehensible game. I was unaware that I was watching the famous Australian Don Bradman and that half the men and boys in Gloucester would have given anything to be in my place!

In retrospect I realise that I also had the experience of seeing the swan-song of a certain era in English country life

– the dismantling of the homes of the gentry before they were sold and turned into hotels or nursing homes, or bought by Arabs. There was a certain sadness about this passing, with the skeleton staff left behind to supervise the sale, the carefully tended gardens beginning to look ragged, the empty stables, the precious furniture heaved out on to the lawn by our rough workmen, and family pictures lying haphazardly in piles on the drive, flattening the grass that was beginning to grow through the gravel. My father liked having me around when he visited a job, and I would sometimes peer into a vast drawing room while the furniture and rugs were carried out to the marquee. When the men finished, there would be nothing left but the chinoisery wallpaper, nothing else to show that a family had once lived there and sat and warmed themselves at the marble fireplace.

"Here," said the foreman one day, and tossed me a teddy bear with one eye that he had found in the drawer of an eighteenth-century bureau. Who had it belonged to? Where was the owner now? I looked at the one remaining eye but it told me nothing. Did that bear know that it had once belonged to a child of the gentry? I had inherited a deep-grained socialism from my father, but just for a moment I felt sympathy for that one-eyed bear and the child who had loved it.

Joe and his merry band were not the only demolishers of this country life; there was also the triumvirate of auctioneer/caterer/antique dealer. The most famous of the dealers was Arthur Negus, who was well known in Gloucester and had been on the radio. "Take my advice," he said to Joe one day, "all this furniture which is going under the hammer for next to nothing will be very valuable one day. Buy a few things now and in a few years you will make a tidy profit."

Joe was never averse to making a profit but at that time money was tight and he didn't take Arthur's advice. However, from time to time he did pick up a few 'ill considered trifles' – items that were unsold at the end of a sale or had been overlooked. Usually they hadn't been bought because they were too unwieldy for the average home, so we acquired several pieces of furniture which were too big for our needs. I remember an enormous oak table which had to be winched through the window to get it into our upstairs living room. Then there was an intricately carved sideboard which was set on two pedestals lined with metal 'to accommodate the champagne'. Such items took up far too much room but Joe liked them and May put up with them for his sake.

Joe's tenting business was thriving as more and more big houses came on the market. He also continued to provide tents for flower shows, gymkhanas and cricket matches, so that together with the takings from May's shop my parents began to recoup the cost of their daring business venture. It was a sunny time in Gloucester in the mid-thirties, with past bitterness forgotten and ahead the promise of a bright future.

But one Sunday morning in September 1939 when May and my sister were in Northgate Methodist chapel listening to the sermon, the preacher broke off and relayed Prime Minister Neville Chamberlain's announcement that Britain was at war with Germany.

CHAPTER 14

War 1939–45

THE OUTBREAK OF this, the second war in the twentieth century, must have been shattering for the men who had survived the earlier 'war to end all war'. At that time the returning soldiers had managed to contain the horrors they had been through with the promise that it would never happen again. My father said very little about the betrayal that Sunday morning, but his looks were grim. The agony was further piled on by news from across the Channel. The Germans had circumvented the French Maginot Line by going through Belgium, meaning that they were able to take over the towns and villages that Joe and his mates had fought for so bitterly twenty-five years previously – Bapaume, Cambrai, Ypres, Somme. It seemed that the blood shed by Joe's generation had been in vain, but worse was to come. Joe listened on the radio to the route of the British Expeditionary Force in France as it retreated to the coast, only a few miles ahead of the pursuing Panzers. In spite of magnificent rear-guard actions by a few suicide companies, the German divisions were unstoppable and the BEF were doomed. With our army lost, we felt that invasion was imminent. As a lover of mine said, "If they come, you will be in a stud farm and I'll be gibbering about in the Highlands."

Then the miracle! A combination of naval vessels and hundreds of little ships and fishing fleets crossed the Channel in May and June 1940 to pluck over 300,000 men off the beaches of Dunkirk. They went on to form the nucleus of a new army which would eventually defeat the enemy. But this defeat would take time and the immediate threat of invasion was only temporarily halted. Throughout the rest of that year and during 1941 and 1942 the threat was maintained and Joe listened to every news bulletin, becoming increasingly agitated and frustrated.

On the home front the minutia of war became part of our lives: ration books, identity cards, the black-out, air-raid wardens and of course the air-raid siren – a long piercing wail which reached a climax and then petered out, "Like a couple of tom cats fighting," my father said.

And now the tent hiring business began to falter. With the future so uncertain no-one wanted to buy houses however magnificent, much less any furniture, so the big marquees remained in their canvas bags under the railway arch. Joe made a little money delivering mail for the GPO with his lorry, but when May worked out his books for 1942 she found that his income had halved.

May and the shop, on the other hand, were thriving. On the food front, many of her farmers brought her off-ration eggs and bacon, and one of the gypsies used to slip her a rabbit from time to time. She also noticed that there was a demand for items to make the Anderson shelters more comfortable. The shelters consisted of corrugated iron sheeting bent into an arch and were supposed to be bomb proof. For families huddled together during an air-raid there was a need for lighting and bedding, so May stocked up with candles, Tilley lamps and sleeping bags. She also installed a large tank of paraffin in the back yard which she sold in half-gallon cans. Then, realising that people needed to black out their windows, she invested in several bales of black material.

Our family didn't use an Anderson shelter but sat in a reinforced part of the brick barn at the back of the house. We would sit there and listen to the bombers going low overhead until chased away by the anti-aircraft fire. "Bastards," said Joe. I found the nearby anti-aircraft fire even more frightening than the bombs.

We still had visitors from Wales, but instead of aunts and uncles it was cousins on their way to their units. There was Nenny from Caerleon, Iolo from Tregaron and Trem from Ogmore. As I saw them off from the Midland Station I wondered what their fates would be. My flamboyant cousin Reginald W Jones turned up one day, travelling in the other direction. Having done well for himself in London he was now attached to some ministry or other and was on his way to St Athan, the air station just outside Cardiff, in his capacity as strategic planner – whatever that meant.

"Don't worry, Auntie May," he said to my mother, "don't bother to cook for me; just a bit of bread and cheese and an onion will do." Now at that time the weekly cheese ration was a square inch cube and onions were unobtainable. "Shows the lifestyle of these civil servants," sniffed my mother when he had gone.

Ever the showman, Reg converted his middle name from William to Winston. I had a birthday card from him once, signed with his adopted name.

Joe continued to be concerned with his business prospects, but some of his associates were faring even worse. He heard a rumour that the catering firm George's, which owed him money, was likely to go bankrupt. In a bankruptcy case the firm's assets are frozen and later apportioned to the various creditors, but there is often not enough money to pay the creditors in full. The canny Welshman in Joe was aware of that. One of the last jobs he and George's did together was to supply the tents and catering for a Cathedral garden party. As soon as it was over and before George's had cleared their stuff, Joe moved in with his lorry and piled up their trestles, linen and cutlery in lieu of payment. In the rush he also nicked a few Cathedral chairs which had slots in the back to take hymn books. I still have some of them, along with a set of knives and forks with 'G' stamped on the handles. Whether they are ill-gotten gains or a reward for opportunism, I have never been able to resolve.

The war dragged on and even seemed to worsen. The Germans held the Channel Islands and the coasts of Holland and France, so they were only twenty-six miles from Dover! In the north they had invaded Norway so that the eastern coast of Scotland was at risk. U-boats were regularly sinking British merchant ships in the Atlantic, and fishes were feeding on our desperately needed supplies. Britain's cities were being bombed into rubble by Goering's Luftwaffe and the inhabitants rarely had an unbroken night's sleep. In Gloucester we were fascinated by a story, maybe apocryphal, of a desperate Londoner who got on the first train out of Paddington going west and put up at the Black Dog Inn where Joe had his yard, only to be kept awake all night by the rumble of the troop trains going across the bridge.

We lived above the shop and our sitting room overlooked the main road. Throughout these worrying times my parents would sit in the big bay window in the evenings, watching the military convoys moving towards the coast. Mile after mile of them straggled from inland bases to the ports of Portsmouth and Bristol. I watched my father's frustration as he saw them pass by; men and women in khaki driving an assortment of vehicles from heavy gun carriages to armour-plated cars. He thought of the days when he too had been part of a defending army.

We were all rooted to the wireless since it was our main source of information, and in May 1940 the Secretary of State for War, Anthony Eden, announced the voluntary mobilisation of any men who were too young or too old to join the forces, or who were in reserved occupations. Joe put his name down immediately, thankful to be given the opportunity to serve. May typed out the weekly schedule and Joe distributed it to the men of his section.

Thousands volunteered, and although at first they were called LDVs (Local Defence Volunteers) they later became known as the Home Guard. This was no ramshackle bunch of amateurs as later depicted on TV but a serious second line of defence against the enemy. They learned unarmed combat, evasive tactics, gun control and street fighting. As each platoon operated in its own area, they were able to use local knowledge to spot any infiltrators or parachutists. In the event they weren't needed, but who knows, perhaps their very existence was one of the factors which led the Germans to cancel the invasion.

By now I was back home, my acting career having been ended by the outbreak of war. My last job on the stage had been in Sheffield Civic Theatre playing Amy in *Little Women* opposite a Laurie who was the juvenile lead. In reality he was no juvenile but a greying sixty year old, all the active young men having been called up. My sense of the ridiculous was capped by the announcement that the theatre was to close, so I went to Gloucester Shire Hall and enrolled as a nursing auxiliary. Soon I was travelling each day in my uniform to a military hospital near Cheltenham.

CHAPTER 15

A Short Life
in the Theatre

L OOKING BACK, I realise that my three-year venture into
the theatrical world was curiously reminiscent of my
experiences as a child when attending a variety of schools.
Tredworth School had included an Empire Day celebration in
the school yard, with me draped in a Union Flag declaiming
'My People'. Was this the beginning of my theatre bug? Or
was it much later at Gloucester High School when we went
as a party to see an outdoor production of TS Eliot's *Murder
in the Cathedral* played against a backdrop of the window
of Tewkesbury Abbey ("Chookesbury," as my father used
to say)? I remember the resonant voice of the actor Robert
Speight as Becket – the particular way he had of saying
'mourn' – and the bright colours of the knights when they
stabbed King Henry's 'turbulent priest'.

At sixteen I passed the school matriculation exam and had
begun my first year in the sixth form, but I wasn't happy; I
wanted to work in the theatre. I prevailed upon my mother to
let me enrol as a student with the Winter Gardens Repertory
Company in Cheltenham but the studentship was a rip-off:
£50 of my parent's hard-earned money to do small parts
and paint scenery. The only positive input was from Miss
Scrivener, a retired elocution teacher who gave her services
free. I remember her giving fellow student Isabel Dean and

myself breathing exercises which entailed gulping deep breaths on all fours!

After Cheltenham I went with the same company to their summer season in Tenby for the princely sum of £4 per week, my mother supplementing my expenses. There I met Kenneth Griffiths, a local boy from Penelly who had been brilliant in a school production of *Richard II* and had been lured to join our summer group for nothing. He played Danny in Emlyn William's *Night Must Fall* and each night I stood in the wings, fascinated by that rich Welsh voice. We were both seventeen years old and ambitious; we realised that to get anywhere in the theatre we had to go to London and visit agents.

Once again subsidised by my mother, I shared a flat in Maida Vale (accommodation was easy to find in those days) with Yvonne Pavey, and we set about the daily trek around the theatrical offices. My qualifications were flimsy: no RADA training, only a studentship in a third-rate repertory company in Cheltenham and bit parts in Tenby, but slowly I managed to get work. There were several months in Bournemouth in *Charley's Aunt*, a year at Gravesend at the mouth of the Thames, a season at Worthing, a session at Felixstowe and finally, some time at Sheffield Civic Theatre. One advantage to these far-flung jobs was that we were able to do our initial rehearsals on West End stages during the mornings. Talk about stepping into the shoes of the mighty!

In between theatrical work I worked as an extra at Pinewood Studios in films such as *Gaslight* with Diana Wynyard and Anton Walbrook, an Austrian dandy. As one of his close-ups didn't meet with his approval, he insisted on having it re-done. I happened to be behind him in the shot and I spent several blissful days on full pay waiting for the studio to get round to the re-take.

I was also in a propaganda film dressed in Women's Land Army garb and turning a wheel to open one of the Norfolk Broads. The director was a doubtful character called Widgey Newman and the crew warned me about his predilection for young girls, but whether it was my guardian angel or whether he was off form, I managed to spend an uninterrupted night at the local hostelry.

Several times at another film studio (I believe it was at Borehamwood), I took part in so-called 'trailers'. These were British-made shorts advertising forthcoming full-length films. One I remember doing was for the American film, *The Invisible Man*. I was fashionably dressed and smoking a cigarette, but the trouble was that I had never smoked (and still don't) and didn't even know how to hold the thing. The director was very patient and I managed to be moderately convincing. The shot ended with me twirling round several times, which was finally converted on screen to my disappearance into thin air.

Whilst tramping around London looking for work, I frequently passed the 'theatre which never closed' in Leicester Square. It was a revue theatre, famous for continuing with performances even during the height of the bombing. It specialised in tableaux vivants and managed to get its naked performers round the censor by ensuring that they remained immobile. I was offered a job there once but I turned it down because it didn't fit in with my idea of 'art'!

Exciting though these experiences were, they were not part of my goal. My dream had always been to play in Shakespeare and yet I was constantly being given juvenile comedy roles in plays such as *George and Margaret*, *Blithe Spirit* and *Rookery Nook*. At Pinewood I was even part of a troupe of 'hikers' singing:

I'm happy when I'm hiking,
Pack upon my back.
With a real good friend
To the journey's end
10, 20, 30, 40, 50 miles a day.

The film starred Harry Korris, a music-hall comedian, who was a far cry from my beloved John Gielgud.

During this time the war had impinged very little on me. True, when I was at Felixstowe I met a bedraggled soldier, his battle dress caked with salt, who had arrived from Dunkirk the night before. I was crass enough to offer him free tickets for the theatre when I'm sure he would have preferred a stiff drink! At Gravesend the search-lights traced the night sky and the locals warned that when the planes came they would follow the river to London and that when they came back they would drop off any remaining bombs on the town. At Bournemouth during the run of *Charley's Aunt* the beach was out of bounds and laced with barbed wire. But this was the time of the 'phoney war' and I wasn't the only one who hadn't woken up to the danger we were in. Where on earth was my socialism, where was my patriotism?

On returning to Gloucester after the debacle of Sheffield, I saw how gravely my father viewed the situation and my eyes were opened. This was when I went to the Shire Hall in Westgate Street and joined the Nursing Auxiliary Service. I lived at home and travelled each day on the train to Cheltenham (twelve miles away), where a former workhouse in St Paul's Road had been converted into a hospital. So as well as nursing wounded soldiers, I looked after fragile old ladies who were isolated in the hospital wing of the workhouse. I remember lifting up their sagging old breasts when I gave them bed-baths.

Living at home meant that I could help May in various ways, both in the shop and coping with rations. These were a housewife's nightmare: eggs, meat, cheese, sugar and cooking fat were severely restricted. It was sometimes possible to get dried egg powder which, when reconstituted with water, served instead of the real thing, and some of the more adventurous housewives used it to make cakes, with liquid paraffin instead of cooking oil. Nothing was wasted, even chicken bones were turned into soup and I learned to drink the nutritious water from cooked cabbage – a habit that I still retain. Bananas were non existent but a few oranges managed to arrive in time for Christmas, and one of these at the bottom of a stocking constituted a rare treat. Strangely enough, throughout the whole of the war I don't remember anyone being hungry. Perhaps our stomachs shrank.

CHAPTER 16

Early Problems
with Integration

MAY AND JO had now been residents of Gloucester for twenty years, during which time they had experienced a general strike, a depression and now another war. But what was their social life like during this period? Joe had played down his Welsh connections sufficiently to be accepted by a coterie of small business men who met regularly at the Northgate Vaults at the top of Worcester Street. In those days very few women went to pubs; they were a largely male preserve. Ironically, this one was next to the Congregational chapel where May used to go on Sundays with my sister Sheila.

Although Joe felt that he still had to tread carefully, there had always been a curious ambivalence of attitude between the English in Gloucester and the Welsh on its borders. In spite of ancient resentments on both sides, there was a grudging acceptance of each other which sometimes had surprising results. This is beautifully illustrated by the Gloucestershire poet, Ivor Gurney. He was in WWI when as a private in the 2/5th Glosters, he met up with the 15th Royal Welsh Fusiliers in the ghastly trenches – an experience he described in the following poem:

FIRST TIME IN

After the dread tales and red yarns of the Line
Anything might have come to us; but the divine
Afterglow brought us up to a Welsh colony
Hiding in sandbag ditches, whispering consolatory
Soft foreign things. Then we were taken in
To low huts candle-lit, shaded close by slitten
Oil sheets, and there the boys gave us kind welcome,
So that we looked out as if from the edge of home.
Sang us Welsh things, and changed all former notions
To human, hopeful things. And the next day's guns
Nor any line-pangs ever quite could blot out
That strangely beautiful entry to war's rout;
Candles they gave us and shared over-rations
(Ulysses found little more in his wanderings without doubt).
'David of the White Rock', 'The Slumber Song' so soft, and
that
Beautiful tune to which roguish words by Welsh pit boys
Are sung – but never more beautiful than here under the
gun's noise.

(Gurney suffered from mental illness and was certified insane in
1922. He was committed to Barnwood House mental hospital
in Gloucester. When he tried to escape it was decided that he
should be taken to the City of London Mental Hospital in
Dartford, Kent. He stayed there for 15 years – ever yearning
for his beloved Cotswold Hills – and died in 1937 .)

May hadn't settled in as well as Joe and had very few
friends, having lost touch with the early chapel acquaintances.
Whether it was her natural reserve or a lingering anti-Welsh

attitude in the town, I was never quite sure. She did, however, get to know a nurse from Coney Hill mental hospital through the Ingrams, whose terraced house had been my parents' refuge. Her name was Brady, but I never knew if that was her first or second name. She was an Irish Catholic and used to regale us with stories of life on the wards, and she and May became firm friends. My mother even went to a nurses' dance at the hospital and bought a long dress for the occasion. This was one of the few times when she spent an evening out; for the most part she stayed at home listening to the wireless. But then something occurred that made me revise my acceptance of her as a self-effacing home-biddy.

One afternoon when I was off-duty from the military hospital, I was helping out in the shop in order for my mother to get up-to-date with the accounts. A tall air force officer came in and bought a ball of string, and I noticed that he had a Canadian flash on his shoulder. Some of my patients were from Canada and I recognised the accent as I gave him his change. He must have been in his late fifties and was of a senior rank, possibly a wing commander, yet he seemed nervous. I looked around at the binder twine and rabbit nets, wondering why he found the place intimidating.

"Er, excuse me," he said. "I am looking for a lady that I knew long ago. Her name was Edwards, Violet Edwards. We were together at Blandford camp."

I gulped and quickly looked through the window to where my mother was busy typing, then I suddenly remembered her bedtime stories of barbed-wire fences and larks at midnight.

"I... I'll get her," I said.

When she came into the shop I discreetly left them alone while they spoke for a long time on opposite sides of the counter; then he went away. She never explained the incident to me and I didn't like to ask, but I was left wondering about a potency that had made this man track her down after so many years. Incidentally, he didn't take the ball of string with him.

Some weeks after this, May's friend Brady announced that she was going to get married to an old family friend and asked me to be the sole bridesmaid. The ceremony took place in the Catholic church round the corner. As I followed her to the altar and smelled the incense and listened to the Latin phrases, I hoped my Nonconformism would be strong enough to withstand the blandishments of that alien religion. Brady gave me a beautiful cameo brooch as a bridesmaid's present. After the reception the couple went to Newton Abbot for their honeymoon, leaving May on her own again. She quickly reverted to the solitary evenings listening to the radio, but from time to time I thought about that young woman who had inspired a man to such an extent that he went looking for her after a gap of thirty years.

"...the end of the beginning." (Winston Churchill)

I T WAS 1942 and the tide of war was beginning to turn in our direction. The British and the Americans were moving up through Italy and the British Navy was harassing the ships in the Norwegian fiords and the Atlantic. The 300,000 soldiers who had been rescued from Dunkirk joined an army poised to cross the Channel and recover Europe, supported by the replenished RAF and the Americans.

I was still nursing, but my two-year contract was nearly up and I went to the Shire Hall prepared to renew it. However, half an hour later I came out of the building having been recruited to work in a laboratory 'somewhere in England'! Although the tide was turning, the armed forces had absorbed most of the young men and Britain was chronically short of technicians who could support the small but precious band of scientists. Anyone with a smattering of mathematics was mopped up to fill this gap, and as I had matriculated in maths and science at school I found myself several weeks later boarding a westward-bound train.

My 'somewhere in England' turned out to be a quiet Somerset town called Ilminster. The research branch of Standard Telephones and Cables, formerly of Sidcup in Kent, had been evacuated there and had taken over a former primary school. I was assigned to a laboratory which concentrated on making shorter and shorter radio waves, a process known under the acronym RADAR which enabled Allied pilots to have more mobility when meeting up with German planes.

There were three laboratories and their director was a Mr Ullrich. Was he a Jew? Had he escaped from Germany? I never found out. From time to time we would have delegations from British or American forces to monitor our progress. The work was hard but interesting – and of course it was away from the bombing. For me, the scariest bit was working with half a dozen car batteries wired up to simulate the cockpit of an aircraft. One day I 'shorted' them and the consequent electrical explosion shot me across the room.

But there were compensations: summer in Somerset, golden hills, haymaking; we even had the sea at nearby Lyme Regis! It was easy to forget that there was a war on; it was as if we were in a time capsule. But now as I look back on those carefree days in Ilminster, I realise that as I was climbing Windmill Hill in bare feet or gathering nuts in the country hedges, millions of Jews were being murdered in Auschwitz and Dachau. As yet innocent of these horrors, we even put on a play at the local War Workers Club and I had a short fling with my leading man, a scientist called Christopher Strachey. Quite unexpectedly, my mother travelled all the way to the West Country to see me perform – she who had never bothered to see me in the school play or in my roles in Cheltenham.

As I cycled to work one June morning, I breasted the hill and saw hundreds of planes towing gliders filled with men. They had been pouring across the Channel since 3am to protect the Normandy beaches. It was the beginning of

D-Day, 6 June 1944, the long-awaited second front – the invasion of Europe.

In the former school in Ilminster we continued measuring and recording; I remember spending the following three months up in the roof charting the variability between the cathode and anode of hundreds of valves. But the Allies were slowly pushing the Germans back and we even began to think that the war in Europe might soon be over. That still left Japan, but now my mind was far from the bigger picture – I had fallen in love!

Sometimes I went by train back to Gloucester for a weekend visit, and it was there that I met Deryk. I was waiting at a bus stop in Worcester Street when a drunken soldier lurched towards me. I wasn't frightened, just a little disturbed, but suddenly a tall sailor came between us and told the soldier to go away. I looked into the sailor's blue eyes, thanking him, and he escorted me over the road back to my mother's string shop.

Deryk was a local Gloucester boy whose father was a GWR lorry driver and whose family lived in a small terrace house at the scruffy end of town, next to the park. But he was also an officer in the Fleet Air Arm and was heavily encrusted with gold braid. This combination of glamour and working-class background bowled me over. We were engaged on St Valentine's Day 1945 and married the following Easter at Ilminster. The flowers in the church, which had been decorated for the Easter festival, served for our own ceremony and I idly remembered those words from *Hamlet*:

Thrift, Horatio, thrift! The funeral baked meats
Did coldly furnish forth the marriage tables.

Should I have taken heed, before diving into my own tragi-comedy?

May, Joe and Sheila travelled by train to be present, changing at Chard and wondering at the unfamiliar countryside. Joe grumbled that the wedding should have taken place in Gloucester but May told him to keep quiet. I borrowed a wedding dress from the vicar's wife, an ex-land girl whose whirlwind romance had been the talk of the village. She gave birth on the day of the ceremony and I sent her my wedding bouquet.

We were married a few months before VE Day (the end of the war in Europe). Deryk's next posting, preparatory to going to the Pacific to fight the Japanese, was in Ormskirk in Lancashire, so I applied to be released from my job and join him there. "We wouldn't want to prevent a new wife from joining her husband," said the official unctuously.

The town of Ormskirk was in future prime minister Harold Wilson's constituency and I think I saw him campaigning during the 1945 election – the one that Labour won so resoundingly and that my father 'had waited all his life for'. We had digs in Aughton, a village just outside the town. Our landlady was Mrs Kirby, the widow of the local blacksmith whose empty forge still remained at the top of our lane. Each time she passed it she would look up as if still expecting him to be there.

It was lovely playing at being a housewife – cooking, washing, shopping and sharing the kitchen with Mrs Kirby. She was an indomitable elderly lady who disliked the local vicar. "All he's after is a knife-and-fork tea," she used to say when he went round the parish. But after a few weeks the novelty of domesticity wore off and I began to look for a job.

Liverpool was a short train journey away, and in June 1945 I was lucky enough to be taken on by the University as a laboratory assistant on the strength of my experience in Ilminster. Each day I left Lime Street station and walked up Brownlow Hill to the TA group at the University, marvelling at the barefoot Irish children I saw playing in the street. (TA represented Tube Alloys, itself a code-name for British nuclear research during the war.) My boss was Dr Joseph Rotblat; he had worked with Chadwick at Cambridge and on the Manhattan Project in America. He had also been present at the test of the atomic bomb in Los Alamos. As Joe Rotblat showed me round the University's own cyclotron accelerator, the domed apparatus for accelerating atomic particles, I slowly realised that our TA group was working on nuclear fission.

My life now centred around the Fleet Air Arm Station, a few light chores at home and the lab in Liverpool. I went to a few functions at the airbase and saw an ENSA (Entertainment National Service Association) group performing in one of the hangers. I wondered if my life would have turned out differently if I had stayed in the theatre, but on the whole I was happy with the way my life had evolved and I was still of course head-over-heels in love with my gorgeous new husband.

On 6 August I was in our bedroom getting ready to take the train to work when I heard on the wireless that the Americans had dropped an atomic bomb on Hiroshima in Japan. That morning I had to push my way through a crowd of journalists to get to the lab and Joe Rotblat hurriedly called us together to say that our TA group was working on the *peaceful* use of nuclear fission and had nothing to do with the horror of Hiroshima. Indeed for the next sixty years, right up to the time he died, Dr Rotblat worked for peace, founding a campaign called 'Pugwash' which sought to eliminate the negative consequences of the splitting of the atom. He was a lovely man, a Jew from Poland, but he and his like had uncorked the nuclear genie and nothing they could do would put it back in the bottle again.

CHAPTER 18

The Loved One

O NE SATURDAY AFTERNOON I was hanging out the washing in Mrs Kirby's back yard, when she said, "You look a bit peaky lately."

This was the era before the contraceptive pill. Deryk and I used a 'Dutch Cap'. I don't know why it was called this, perhaps because it fitted over the cervix to prevent any sperm entering the womb. We used it nightly because Deryk was an obsessive (he even filed his handkerchiefs according to size) and from the beginning of the marriage he had decided that we should make love every night. This caused problems because the instructions relative to the cap were that it should be left in for at least twelve hours after intercourse, but this didn't fit in with Deryk's schedule. True, if we made love at 11pm I could take it out after coffee break the following morning, but if we performed later in the night I had to leave it in until the following afternoon and then hurriedly put it back in again for the coming night. I gave up the struggle and left the damn thing in for days on end, sometimes for a whole week.

That Saturday morning I knew that my period was late, but I wasn't unduly worried because they had always been erratic. However, after another two weeks I became apprehensive and left a urine sample with the local doctor, who sent it off to be injected into a female toad. Ten days later the result came back – it was positive. I bought a fruit cake, using up some of our precious rations, and walked back to Mrs Kirby's bungalow as carefully as if I was carrying a pitcher of water. I didn't phone Deryk at work because I thought it better to tell him the good news in our own surroundings.

Deryk had recently acquired a second-hand motorbike which tended to break down, and that evening when he came home he dumped a greasy carburettor on one of Mrs Kirby's immaculate rose-patterned chair covers.

"I had to beg a lift home," he said testily. "Bloody bike!"

I took a deep breath, feeling as if I was giving this man I loved a most treasured possession. What were those lines from WB Yeats' poem?

I have spread my dreams under your feet;
Tread softly because you tread on my dreams.

"I'm pregnant," I said.

There was a pause.

"Are you sure?" he asked.

"Absolutely. The doctor has given me forms for milk and rose-hip syrup."

"What happened?"

I looked up.

"What do you mean?"

"What happened, what went wrong?"

Wrong!

"I don't know," I said laughing, pouring out the tea, "perhaps the sperm swam up over the Wellington boot."

He didn't laugh and ignored the precious fruit cake. Maybe I shouldn't have sprung it on him so suddenly, maybe

I should have waited until the right moment. What was it the women's magazines always stressed? "At such a time your husband needs the reassurance of your love!" I had been clumsy and insensitive.

"You'll have to get rid of it," he said.

I was bewildered.

"How do you mean, get rid of it?"

"Just that. I don't want it."

He picked up the carburettor, leaving a greasy mark on the roses, and went into the back kitchen.

He didn't mean it, I thought, he was tired and the motorbike was giving him trouble. Tomorrow would be different.

He came to bed late.

"I'm sorry about the contraceptives," I said. "I can't think how it happened."

"Well you've certainly got us into something now!"

"I suppose so, but we were going to have children some time. It's just, well, a bit sooner…"

"This isn't a world to bring a child into."

"But…"

"The air is polluted, the West is a mess — ruined cities, people living like rats."

"But not here, not where we are. Anyway life has to go on."

He savagely tied his pyjama cord.

"Typical woman, only thinking of yourself. I'm thinking of a child brought into this world that we have just made such a mess of. It's irresponsible, it's criminal."

We didn't make love that night. He got into bed and turned his back on me. I should have been shattered but I went to sleep and dreamt of nursery rhymes. Tomorrow would be different.

But it wasn't. Deryk was adamant and his arguments seemed unanswerable. It was an uneven battle – logic against sentiment – and I lost. Remember the times we were living in: men were the dominant species and women were expected to be subjugated to them. Years later I realised that the problem had not so much been a baby, but an *unplanned* baby. Nature had disturbed the filing system; a handkerchief was out of place.

CHAPTER 19

The Unloved One

O N 2 SEPTEMBER 1945, after a second atomic bomb
had been dropped on Nagasaki, General Douglas
MacArthur accepted the Japanese surrender in Tokyo Bay.
The war was over.

The same day I went into a chemist's shop in Ormskirk
and bought 100 tablets of quinine. The bottle lay in my
pocket like a time-bomb as I walked home. Italian prisoners-
of-war were lifting potatoes in the flat Lancashire fields, filling
the sacks and then loading them on to a horse-drawn cart.
I supposed that they would soon be going home, home to
their wives, home to make babies. The grey Shire horse stood
patiently in the sunshine, blinking flies from its eyes.

I took two or three tablets but nothing happened. Then
I started taking them in tens – still nothing. It was very
depressing going to the loo and hoping for a welcome show
of blood.

"Try laxatives," said Deryk.

I took enough senna pods to purge a hippopotamus, but
all that happened was an acute attack of diarrhoea. Deryk
looked up from tinkering with the bike.

"You don't try hard enough," he said, wiping Swarfega
off his hands.

I was now over three months pregnant; the milk ducts were
being activated and my nipples were sore. I read books in the

library and tried to remember odd bits of information that I had acquired. Oestrogen came into it somewhere but what it was, how one got it and what effect it had, I didn't know. I tried hot baths with potassium permanganate in them but all that happened was that I stained Mrs Kirby's bath blue. I tried hotter baths after having swallowed half a bottle of gin and came out like an inebriated turkey – but nothing shifted.

"We'll go to Southport," said Deryk loftily one Saturday, "that should fix it."

Southport had sea, Southport had sands, but above all Southport had a fun-fare and I went on the Big Dipper three times running. I had always hated slides, even the small ones in children's playgrounds, so that at the end of the afternoon I was green and sick – and still pregnant!

We went home to Gloucester for Christmas and our families moved in with advice:

"Be sure to take the rose-hip syrup."

"Don't lift any heavy weights."

"Rest every afternoon."

And from my mother-in-law: "Don't knit too many first sizes."

My doting godfather offered his house and his daily woman for the big event. How could I tell him that we didn't want it? Indeed, how could I say it when it wasn't true on my part? By now I could feel the baby inside me. Travelling back to Lancashire on the bike, we stopped at a transport café for a break. I sipped the scalding hot tea and said tentatively, "Perhaps we should have it after all."

"We've gone into that," said Deryk. "How can any rational people bring a child into an irrational world!"

"I know, but what can I do? I've tried everything."

As I climbed with difficulty onto the pillion seat he continued, "I'll tell you this. The moment it is born I'll leave you."

"But why? Everyone has babies; it may turn out very nice."

Deryk hit the roof.

"Nice! A typical selfish attitude. What do you think we are? Animals? You're giving in to the basic of human instincts, on a level of slobbering and grunting in the farmyard. You're not the girl I married. You've changed and I tell you, you'll bring it up alone. I won't be there."

He kicked the starter motor and with a jerk we zoomed off northwards.

Why didn't I call his bluff? Why did I decide to try and cope with it alone? Why didn't I talk to someone – my mother or my godfather? In those days marriage was a curious set-up; it was as if on the day of the flowers, the hymns and the champagne a woman walked into a glass box. The only other person in my glass box was Deryk and he was implacable. What did he really feel? Where did he get the strength to be so determined? By now I was scared and maybe he was scared too, but it didn't make him waver; he was trapped in a stance of rigidity. The weeks went by, I was now four and a half months gone and I didn't think I could face any more days of Deryk coming home from the air station and saying, "Well?"

"I'm sorry, nothing."

"Christ Almighty, have I married a woman or a moron? You're trying to get away with it, aren't you! I tell you, if you go through with this I'll make sure that you regret it for the rest of your life!"

I broke my self-imposed silence and wrote to my friend Joan. She had been my best friend at school and a bridesmaid at my wedding; moreover she was a trained nurse. I asked her how I could terminate the pregnancy and she came up from Gloucester right away to see me.

"We just don't feel we have the right to bring a child into this world," said Deryk with his back to the kitchen range.

Joan listened and asked a few questions about periods, morning sickness and heartburn.

"It's well over four months," she said. "It could be dangerous."

"Nonsense," said Deryk, "that's a myth put out by the Catholics."

Later, when we were washing up in the kitchen, Joan turned to me and said, "Forget Deryk. What do you want?"

"I don't want it," I said unhesitatingly. Was it my imagination or did I actually hear a cock crow?

Joan tried another tactic.

"You know that by now it will be well formed, with pink fingers and toenails?" (This was before they had developed any scanning techniques, so I hadn't been offered a sight of the foetus.)

"I don't care," I said bravely, "I've made up my mind."

Joan was due back in Gloucester on duty the following day. My last words to her were that if she didn't help me, I'd try and find a local abortionist. This convinced her as I had cunningly calculated it would, so against her better judgement she sent me some of the pills which the hospital used to induce labour, saying that they would take effect within three days. She still pleaded for me to think again before committing myself to such a drastic act.

I took the pills and waited. It was now late January 1946 and some days were beginning to smell of spring. The earth was stirring with new life, yet I who had so often identified with nature was about to brutally wrench myself away from it. I don't remember what Deryk was doing at this time; he was a shadowy figure and I'm not even sure if I cooked his meals. I was cocooned in the body I had betrayed and I hoped that I would die.

Two nights later the sac of water in which the baby was swimming broke and flooded Mrs Kirby's second-best bed. Deryk was embarrassed by the episode and went off to work in the morning leaving me to clear up and wash the sheets. I was alone in a nightmare. As I turned the mangle I thought of the sentient being inside me which had been alive and which I had sentenced to death. Again I hoped to die.

Labour pains started at night a few days later. Deryk phoned the doctor who told him to phone again when the pains were at five-minute intervals. I hadn't experienced such pain before; there had been toothaches and period pains but the ones that night were all-embracing. I was enfolded in them and taken up to an intense white plateau where gulls screeched and tore the air. I writhed and twisted and Deryk sat on the edge of the bed awkwardly with his boots on.

"It's snowing," he said.

I didn't answer but turned again to look at the bloody clock. Deryk picked it up and turned it round to face the wall.

"I'll get you some tea," he said with surprising gentleness.

The bedroom had very little furniture and no ornaments, just a bedside table with a light and a wickerwork shade which threw patterns on Mrs Kirby's ceiling. With the clock gone those patterns were all I had to look at between pains. Deryk came back with the tea but I didn't want any, I just lay there waiting for the next terrifying lift to the white plateau. Then I heard screaming, but it wasn't the gulls.

"I'll go and get the doctor now," said Deryk. His voice was young and frightened.

When he had gone, the pain lessened and I felt that my muscles were trying to push. Obeying some instinct I got out of bed and sat on the chamber pot. A terrible chill enveloped my whole body; surely this was death, the chill of death! I remembered the words of the landlady in Shakespeare's *Henry V* describing Falstaff's death:

"... his feet ... were as cold as any stone. Then I felt to his knees, and so up'ard and up'ard, and all was as cold as any stone."

I sat on the white chamber pot which was pattered with roses and thought of the fat knight who "a' babbled of green fields," as he died. Perhaps birth and death are inter linked and when a woman gives birth she is also very close to death. My body gave a final push, and as the two men came in through the door my son left my body.

"I see, wrong time," said Deryk, embarrassed.

What a joke! What an appalling joke! I was laughing as they helped me back onto the bed.

The doctor was no fool; we had after all been sailing very close to the wind and he didn't want any unnecessary bureaucracy to result from our criminal stupidity. He was polite to me, even kind; he expelled the placenta and cleaned me up, then curtly turned to Deryk and told him to burn the garbage in the kitchen range. Then he left.

Much later, Deryk came back into the room. He looked green and I was reminded of Joan's warning about rosy-tipped fingers and toe-nails.

The marriage continued for the next twenty-five years. It had to; its continuation had been bought with the price of a burnt offering.

The other price was a band of ice around my heart which never melted and which prevented me from having a close association with any other human being for the rest of my life.

CHAPTER 20

Looking Ahead,
and a Funeral

B UT WOMEN ARE notoriously resilient, and I was
determined to make a go of the marriage that had cost
so much. I felt it incumbent on me to do so if only to make
sense of that dreadful night in Mrs Kirby's second bedroom.
Deryk continued with his usual routine, going to the airbase on the bike and tinkering with it most evenings while I
continued at Liverpool University.

But events beyond our own domestic problems took
over as the war in the Pacific came to an end. This time the
celebrations were muted because we realised that when the
Americans dropped the atomic bombs on Japan a new and
dreadful era had begun for the world. The many scientists
who had developed the bomb had been against its actual use,
arguing that the practice demonstration at Los Alamos should
have been enough to convince the Japanese to surrender. But
in spite of the doubts about the ethics of how the war ended,
the realisation that the damn thing was over was a reason
to rejoice. No more sirens, no more bombings, no more
blackouts, and Deryk didn't have to go to fight the Japanese.

A by-product of these world events was a softening of
Deryk's attitude to having children, so when a few years
later I became pregnant (that damn cap again!) he offered no
resistance. Maybe he had run out of excuses or he began to

realise that he lacked a son. Perhaps he felt that the world was now a more suitable place for children. But he was still the old obsessive and when the first child turned out to be female he stomped around the house and refused to speak to me for days after the confinement. It was a lonely time mitigated only by the fact that my daughter Jenny was a roly-poly baby. At two years old she was charmingly short and stocky. "She's like a little pitter," said my father, remembering his days with the sturdy pit ponies.

After the thanksgiving services for the end of the war which took place across the country from the mighty St Paul's to the smallest Hebridean chapel, the British went wild in spite of guilt about the bomb. Enormous bonfires were lit and there were street parties galore. All the forgotten flower shows, steeple chases and cricket matches were resurrected. My mother sold hundreds of Union Jacks and Joe's tenting business, which had been barely viable during the war, was now inundated with enquiries.

"You'll have to get bigger premises," said May.

"What?" said Joe, aghast. "Do you mean move?"

"We must. And not too far from town. I've already had to turn down several enquiries."

Urged on by May, Joe hunted around for a place which would be roomier than the one under the railway arch. Eventually he found a half-acre plot with planning permission to erect a warehouse. It was at Longford, a small suburb two miles from the city. The access was good and there was plenty of space for him to park his lorry and the car.

"That tree will have to come down," said a friendly architect who was drawing up plans for the warehouse.

"I can't kill a tree," said Joe, as memories of a childhood

on the barren Welsh mountains came back to him. He refused to budge and the plans had to be redrawn while May fumed at the extra expense. But she let him have his way. "After all," she said, "he doesn't ask a lot out of life." Did she have a strange inkling about how soon that life would come to an end?

May and Joe were now in their sixties and May was feeling the strain of running the shop on her own, so she employed an assistant. His name was Victor and he was slightly crippled with one leg shorter than the other. It was typical of my mother that she was prepared to take on someone who would have had trouble finding employment elsewhere. In spite of his handicap he was active enough to handle the camping equipment which May had begun to promote. I remember the distinctive smell of the waterproofed canvas coming from the small tents which were stacked behind the shop. The prewar craze for the outdoor life had resurfaced and youngsters set off for the hills with their one or two-man tents, sleeping safely under the tranquil skies.

With extended premises at Longford, Joe was also able to take on more work. Although the end-of-war excitement had eventually died down, traditional village fetes and horse shows continued. The sale of grand houses picked up and Joe's marquees graced many more expansive front lawns. He still employed his casual labourers or their sons, but there were no butlers to bring them tea from the servants' quarters because domestics were no longer prepared to work for peanuts. Life had become more utilitarian and less deferential – the old social distinctions had given way to the cult of money.

Like May, Joe added a permanent member of staff to his set of casuals. Mr Fred Merrit was quartered in the completed warehouse and repaired the tents when they came back after shows. For example, a marquee in Gloucester Park suffered a gash in its side where an elephant from Cotteral's Circus had lumbered into it. Fred was far more amenable than Mr Fudge had been and Joe enjoyed working with him so much that he even considered leaving him something in his will! When my father mentioned this to me I wondered if he was beginning to have certain intimations of mortality. Even if he did, the last few years of his life were very cheerful rather than gloom-laden, though May thought he was taking on too much.

Joe liked travelling around the Cotswolds in his newly-bought lorry and enjoyed the companionship of his work force. He looked forward to evenings of discussion in the Northgate Vaults at the top of Worcester Street. He felt able to talk about socialism now and often quoted the *Daily Herald* to clinch his arguments. But one day after a busy week – cricket in the grounds of Cheltenham College, a sale at Toddington Hall mansion and a craft fair in Gloucester Park – the hardships of his early life took their toll. On the way back from checking out the marquees in the park he had a heart attack. He was taken to Gloucester Royal Infirmary but died peacefully after a few days, content that he was being looked after by the new Labour Government and the recently-established NHS founded by Aneurin Bevan.

"I would have liked a few more years," he told me as he lay in the hospital bed. To my mind that was as good a sentiment as any on which to die.

The Welsh came up for the funeral which took place at the crematorium in Cheltenham. Some were brought by Bill Coal and his wife Martha in their Standard Vanguard, with Martha's brother Howard Harries driving. Simon John, Joe's brother from Hendre Post, also came. The small chapel resounded to male voices singing 'Ar Hyd y Nos' and Joe's ashes were later set behind a plaque in the wall. After the funeral the hill farmers from Gilfach Goch in Blackmill and ex-miners from Ogmore Vale sat around the over-large oak table in our upstairs sitting room and reminisced about 'good old Joe', the price of milk, and Wales's chances against the All Blacks at Cardiff Arms Park.

As an epitaph, you could say that although Joe had made a successful career as a businessman, he never attained the promise of his youth. But perhaps that promise was achieved by his stubborn determination to succeed in a foreign country for the sake of his family. And what of his socialism? It did not die with him, for I was able to pick up the banner after eventually freeing myself from a failed marriage. I answered the call of President Samora Machel to socialists worldwide to go to Mozambique and help develop his newly-independent country.

Having no son to carry on after him, Joe had already arranged the disposal of the tenting business so when he died May was left a comparatively rich widow. She fulfilled a long-cherished ambition and bought a house on the Estcourt Road, a new development at the posh end of Gloucester. (May, bless her, was prone to delusions of grandeur, probably as a result of the discrimination she had experienced.) She tried to follow the middle-class suburban life but the boredom of living in an opulent backwater didn't suit this feisty woman and in less than a year she moved with my sister to a flat in the centre of Gloucester. Sheila began a two-year teacher-training course at a college in Kidderminster and later graduated as a primary school teacher. Meanwhile, I was studying part-time for a degree while I doggedly carried on trying to make the best of things with Deryk.

CHAPTER 21

Oxford

A FEW MONTHS after VJ Day when Joe was still alive, my husband was formally demobbed and we had to consider his future. Before he joined up he had been a Post Office engineer but he wasn't keen on returning to that job. Indeed he tried to stay on in the navy but the authorities turned him down as he was deemed to be 'largely antagonistic to discipline' according to his final appraisal. He then suggested to my father that he might join the firm but Joe diplomatically refused, explaining that Deryk was "too much of a gentleman." I wonder what that phrase was a code for in Ogmore-speak? I was puzzled by these rejections of my handsome hero. Why couldn't they see his undoubted qualities? I was of course still more or less in love! However, a solution was waiting for us.

A grateful nation decided to reward its returning forces with the offer of education so Deryk and I, prompted by my doting godfather who believed that I had married beneath myself, trekked around the Oxford colleges until he was eventually accepted by the comparatively new St Catherine's. I was delighted that my plan of rescuing this gorgeous creature from working-class oblivion was succeeding beyond my wildest dreams. We settled into a house on the Berkshire border five miles from the centre of Oxford.

Unfortunately, it didn't work. Deryk seemed incapable of studying and did so badly in his exams that his course was extended from two to three years. Meanwhile, the University had decided that the influx of mature ex-soldiers with dubious qualifications needed help to get through their studies, so volunteers from the normal student population were paired with the ones who were struggling. Deryk's mentor was a young third year zoology student called Anne McLaren (who became a family friend and godmother to my first child, Jenny) but even she couldn't lift him from the morass in which he found himself.

I was so frustrated watching Deryk waste his amazing opportunity that I reverted to my old love – the theatre. On the strength of my previous experience I was invited to join OUDS (Oxford University Dramatic Society) and was at last able to act in some of the classics rather than modern farce. At Oxford I was Emilia in *Othello*, Yelena in *Uncle Vanya*, the Green Woman in *Peer Gynt* and Gertrude in *Hamlet*. I also met many of the greats before they became famous: John Schlesinger, Tony Richardson, Ken Tynan and so on. I was even congratulated on a particular mime by a visiting French director called Michele St Denise!

But I didn't forget the real reason why we were in Oxford and I helped Deryk as much as I could with his studies after Anne had graduated and left. Although the level of the Physics syllabus was far beyond me, I knew the jargon from my time in Ilminster. For three months before his finals I went through back papers in the Sheldonian Library and gave him what I predicted might be the questions. Did it help? I will never know.

I loved Oxford with its dreaming spires and in spite of the worry about Deryk, I was able to soak up its history and environment – the Martyr's Memorial, Merton College quad, the Pitt Rivers Museum, the Bodleian Library and punts on the Isis and Cherwell.

At the end of the summer term of 1949 there was a gradual exodus of the war combatants. One of the University magazines called *Cherwell* had the following headline in bold capitals on its front cover: "KISS THE BOYS GOODBYE". Oxford then reverted to normality.

CHAPTER 22

The End of the Marriage

D ERYK CAME OUT with a third class honours degree which wasn't even good enough to get into the atomic energy plant at Harwell, a few miles away from our rural retreat. He returned to the Post Office but as a sop he was transferred to their Dollis Hill Research Station. We kept the house near Oxford and used it as a weekend retreat from the rather dull North London suburb of Neasden. It was there that I had two more girls (more huffing and puffing from Deryk), Penny and Veronica.

It was lovely having a little family and playing at being a housewife but money was tight, maintaining two houses was difficult, and I began to get restive. I took on a job in the statistics branch of a nearby plastics factory in London and revived their dying amateur dramatic society. We even put on a play! But this couldn't overcome the frustration of watching Deryk travel every day to a dead-end job, so I took a two-year teacher-training course, driving each day to South London in a recently acquired veteran Austin Seven. I ended up as a mathematics teacher in Holland Park Comprehensive School in Kensington.

This latest venture of mine spelt the end of our twenty-year-old marriage. Deryk resented my new independence and hated anything to do with the school and its trendy clientele. He tried his best to stop me carrying on, often endeavouring to prevent me from getting to work on time. The crunch came one Sunday evening when we were in our rural retreat and I was getting things ready for our return to London the following day. Deryk became deliberately obstructive and I realised that he had no intention of getting me or the two children (Jenny was at university) back in time. Suddenly I snapped and ordered a taxi to take me and the girls to Didcot station. I found that there was a train already in and it was going east to the capital. I stolidly watched it depart in a cloud of steam and waited for the next one which was going in the opposite direction – to Gloucester! My sister answered the door as if an absconding sibling was nothing out of the ordinary, and fixed us up with blankets and pillows.

The next morning, sitting on the sofa and listening to the two girls in the kitchen teaching May how to make flapjacks, I pondered on what I had just done. I'd left my husband; I'd walked out of a house leaving behind the milestones of my life – the books, the silver tea-service from my godfather, the furniture from the woodcarver in Watlington, the children's Noah's Ark and animals, the rose bush by the back window which was just coming into bud, and above all my trusty 1937 Austin Seven car. Would I ever see them again?

I thought back over the last twenty years and allowed myself for once to look clearly at the man with whom I had shared them. He was arrogant and had destructive tendencies, he had forced me to get rid of my son and had subsequently tried to destroy me as a person. But then, quixotically, he had undergone a *volte-face* over the following three pregnancies. With new clarity of memory I realised that he had also isolated me from the people I loved. Throughout our marriage he had tried to wean me away from my Welsh connections. I remember in the first flush of pride I had taken my handsome husband to Heatherville to show him off, but he must have hated the experience because we never went again. He was polite to my parents but after Joe had tactfully refused to incorporate him in Smith & Sons we rarely visited them. He must have found it the ultimate betrayal when I walked out of his house and went back to my mother and sister.

The girls and I stayed with them for a week and then went back to London, checking in temporarily at a hotel. Holland Park School, as well as being the first London comprehensive, had a staff room which was a thriving market place. The history teacher, Graham Hollister-Short, put me up for a few weeks, having himself just emerged from a failed relationship; I bought a second-hand car from Harry the geography teacher; and I took over a nearby mews cottage from Linda the divinity teacher whose father had bought her a house.

Meanwhile, events in Gloucester were moving rapidly. My sister got married to a man from the Midlands and continued with her job in the local school. May arranged for the newly-weds to buy a house on the outskirts of the town, moving in with them so that she could help Sheila. It worked well at first but May found this cosy solution boring and began to get itchy feet. She realised that Joe's death had freed her from the Goldsworthy tentacles, so when a member of the Edwards family died she decided to go to his funeral in Tregaron.

The Welsh are good at funerals. It is something to do with the Protestant ethic, harmonised singing, and of course the opportunity to meet relatives and have a good old gossip. As well as being introduced to several cousins with whom she had lost touch, May met Sam Harcombe at the funeral. He had been married to Enid, another Edwards, who had died two years previously. Sam was a retired naval scientist but still lived in Portsmouth where he had worked for the Admiralty.

May learnt that he was a Freemason and that he was also influential in the Portsmouth Welsh Society.

I don't know what particularly attracted May to him. Was it his status or was it really (as she told me later) the chance to get away from my domineering husband? (Although I had left Deryk he was still liable to turn up and cause havoc.) In any event they were married three months after meeting in Tregaron and May moved to his big rambling house on the outskirts of Portsmouth with a book-lined library and Spode china dinner plates. As Sam's wife she became an accepted member of the Welsh Society and was invited to various do's or *Noson Lawen* (jolly evenings), making her feel obliged to buy a few more long dresses. (I have a photograph of her sitting beside Sam at a dinner table with the great and good of Portsmouth on either side.) She was now in her element having achieved through marriage the vicarious elevated status to which she had so often aspired.

But sadly the glory didn't last. Sam became ill and May, true to her vows, nursed him through a difficult illness until he died and was laid out in the library. For the first time in my life I witnessed an open coffin lying on a trestle with the occupant dressed in white and looking beatific.

Sam had requested that his body be cremated in Portsmouth and his ashes taken to Llanwonno, a tiny village high above the Rhondda Fawr valley. May travelled there on the overnight train and eventually arrived at the only pub. Tea had been ordered and relatives had come from as far away as Ynys Môn (Anglesey) to attend the ceremony. Unfortunately, May had forgotten to pick up the ashes from Portsmouth crematorium. When this omission was discovered there was general consternation. I arrived at Llanwonno and was met by Tom, Sheila's husband.

"I'm afraid Sam's not here," he said laconically.

Some of the guests suggested that the ashes could be flown by chartered flight from Portsmouth to Cardiff but this was dismissed as too expensive and too late. The tea had already been paid for so it was agreed to carry on with the secular part of the day. We sat down to Welsh cakes and buttered *bara brith* while the Minister spoke a few words in appreciation of Sam Harcombe, the boy from Tregaron, concluding with a passing reference to the unfortunate circumstance of his ashes. I had the feeling that when the disappointed mourners returned home and told their separate tales, a ripple of laughter spread across the Principality! May was highly embarrassed and returned a week later with the casket which was put beside Sam's first wife, Enid.

May was now on her own again in the rambling Portsmouth house and as Sam's grown-up children hadn't taken kindly to his second marriage, her sense of isolation increased. It was time to move on. She returned to Gloucester and moved back into my sister's house. Sheila now had two small children so May settled into the role of grandmother and helped with the cooking and cleaning while Sheila went to work in the local primary school. May also enjoyed the company of an old family friend called Ida. She was unmarried, sixty-ish and had known my parents since she was a child, having lived next door to one of the many furnished rooms they had rented when they were trying to get established. Ida spoke fondly of my father so May felt comfortable with her.

Meanwhile in London my divorce was in full swing. Most divorces are unpleasant but this one was particularly nasty and I had to endure a mauling from the opposing barrister. My barrister was a Welshman, Peter Morgan from Merthyr Mawr in Glamorgan. "We haf to recofer our lost terr-it-oree," he said in his lilting voice. "We need a clo-ose relatif to put your side to the chudge."

I rang Gloucester and suggested that Sheila's husband Tom could come up and testify for me. Tom was charming but spineless and the thought of standing up at the Old Bailey terrified him. My mother overheard and put down the pan of chips she was cooking. "Find out the time of the next train to Paddington," she said, reaching for her coat.

I will never forget the sight of this feisty eighty-year-old standing in Court No. 2 at the Old Bailey: clear-voiced, defiant and commanding respect from all around her.

I got my divorce of course, with costs.

CHAPTER 23

An Indian Summer

FOR THE NEXT few years while Sheila was teaching at Barnwood School, May helped to run the house and sometimes went to stay with her cousins in Newport at weekends. There she established a firm friendship with two of my elderly and widowed aunts, Gwladys and Margaret. One day the three of them decided to go on holiday together. I was living in London at the time, teaching in Holland Park School, so I put them up on their way to Heathrow. I was intrigued by their dissimilarity. Auntie Gwladys was softly spoken and timid (my mother told me that she was dominated by her daughter Molly) whereas Auntie Margaret was a large lady with flamboyant clothes and a big voice. The third of the trio, my mother, was softly spoken like Gwladys but with a steel-like determination.

Their first outing was a Saga holiday to France but later they became more daring and took holiday packages to Greece and Turkey. It was heartening to see these elderly ladies enjoying themselves after their far from easy lives, but time was not on their side. Two and a half years after their first holiday together Gwladys died and Margaret became bedridden, leaving May on her own for the third time. She took the loss of her fellow travellers very well and seemed well-nigh indestructible herself, but then Sheila and I noticed that she had begun to slow down a little and she had one or two bad falls.

"It always seems to happen on the Cross," May said.

Gloucester Cross is where four streets meet: Northgate, Southgate, Eastgate and Westgate, with the squat tower of St Michael's Church at the centre. This is the business heart of Gloucester and perhaps May used to daydream as she passed the bank, the watchmaker's and Beard's Bookshop. Whatever the reason for her unsteadiness, Sheila and I began to think of a solution but before we could articulate it even to each other, May was there before us.

"I think I'll move to a home," she said. "I'd like to have a few more people of my own age to talk to."

There were two retirement homes on our side of Gloucester. One was posh, the other less so. May opted for the posh one at first – it was the Estcourt Road syndrome all over again. She stayed there for several months but the pretentiousness of the place and the people did not suit her. My mother may have had mild delusions of grandeur but she also had a socialist background which eventually prevailed. She moved to the more modest Methodist home at the top of Denmark Road which was close to my old school and overlooked some pretty public gardens. This was to be the final move in her long life and possibly the most successful.

May was in her element with the mix of residents – retired schoolteachers, widows of successful shopkeepers, ex-nurses – most of whom lived on modest pensions. Relatives and friends visited, including the faithful Ida, and they didn't feel intimidated as they had been by the grandeur of the surroundings in the first home. May took over the running of the library and transformed it, reorganising the books and instituting a more professional system of lending. She also contacted the Methodist Central Office for specific books which the residents sometimes requested. Soon the small space which had been put aside for the library began to be known as Mrs Goldsworthy's room.

In moving to a home run by a Methodist foundation, May's faith had come full circle from the Primitive Methodist Chapel by the shallow river in Wales to this comfortable retreat in England. Once a week a young minister would come and take a service and the residents would sing hymns accompanied by an ancient harpsichord. Did May remember the 'Prim' and the Sunday schools she used to take? Did she remember the early days in Gloucester when she spoke at a Methodist function in the forest? "Lead kindly light," sang the residents, and May joined in with pride.

When tea and cake were served by the staff after the service, May began to notice that the young minister took a double helping of cook's Victoria sandwich. Was he going hungry? "Of course they don't get paid very much," she reasoned, so she made sure that in the following weeks she put a bigger coin in the collection box.

Sheila and I were very pleased to see our mother so happy. However, happiness does not necessarily prolong life and when she became too infirm to be cared for by the home she was transferred to an annex of Gloucester Royal Infirmary in Horton Road. Every time I came down from London to see her I would bring a miniature bottle of sherry which I bought on the train from Paddington. She would give me her old smile and indicate that she would like a sip. I would help her to sit up. One day she lay back on the pillow and closed her eyes, not seeing me as I tip-toed from the room. The hospital phoned us early next morning to say that she had died peacefully in her sleep, so Sheila and I went to say farewell.

CHAPTER 24

Funeral of a Great Lady

SHEILA AND I both felt that my mother's life warranted a little more than the usual obsequies, so we went to see the local chaplain of the RAFVR (Royal Air Force Voluntary Reserve) and explained that our mother had been in the Royal Flying Corps. He immediately offered to help with the cremation service.

"Would you like to choose a couple of hymns?" he asked. Sheila suggested 'The Lord's my Shepherd' and I thought we could finish with 'Ar Hyd y Nos'. I was tempted to include 'Caersalem', the hymn with which I have always associated my mother, but I chickened out. I knew that those opening lines would find me a crumpled heap on the tiled floor.

"It is usual for a member of the family to give a few final words," he said, looking pointedly at me as the eldest. I had been trained in the theatre and was used to speaking before an audience but I felt I could not trust myself in this most poignant situation; my voice would falter or tears would overwhelm me.

"I'd rather leave it to you," I said, "but maybe I could give you a poem to read out."

I have always admired the succinctness of WH Auden and I chose some verses from *Funeral Blues*, one of the best things he ever wrote.

Stop all the clocks, cut off the telephone,
Prevent the dog from barking with a juicy bone,
Silence the pianos and with muffled drum
Bring out the coffin, let the mourners come.

She was my North, my South, my East and West,
My working week and my Sunday rest,
My noon, my midnight, my talk, my song;
I thought that love would last for ever; I was wrong.

I copied the verses out carefully on a clean sheet of paper
and sent it to the chaplain in time for the ceremony, but he
politely rejected it as "not suitable". I wonder what he meant
by that phrase? Did he disapprove of the very left-wing,
agnostic Auden, or was the poem not holy enough for him?
Many years later I went to see the film *Four Weddings and a
Funeral* and the funeral service featured my rejected poem. I
wonder, do chaplains ever go to the pictures?

Although May's crematorium service proceeded without
the benefit of Auden, it was impressive in other respects. The
coffin was carried by four ex-RAF men and was draped with a
Union Jack. The congregation, which included representatives
of the Methodist home and the faithful Ida (most of the Welsh
relatives being either dead or dying), sang well but there was
none of the verve or the *hwyl* that we heard at Joe's funeral.
However, the burly pall-bearers weighed in with gusto even
though they mispronounced some of the Welsh words.

There was a correspondent from *The Citizen* at the door
of the chapel and that evening the paper gave details of the
cremation ceremony. The article spoke of May as "one of
the last women who served in the First World War," and

included a picture of her in uniform. So in death my mother was accorded the respect which she had always craved in life and Sheila and I were left proud but desolate.

This scamper through the twentieth century has been an account of two people I loved. From one angle their lives were uneventful ("Nothing to write home about," as my mother used to say) but they illustrate the great courage inherent in the Welsh as a people – the way they stick to a task and make the best of difficult circumstances. May and Joe stayed true to this tradition even though they would have been the last to admit it. As my cousin Bill says, "There must have been something in those genes," because the tradition lives on.

Billie, the grandson of my uncle Simon Goldsworthy, became leader of the Welsh Farmers' Union and was awarded an OBE. (I remember an English equivalent getting a knighthood. Was this a lingering discrimination?)

Auntie Gwen's son Reginald Winston Jones made a packet out of tailoring with several shops in London's West End.

I tried and failed to be a Socialist MP but then became a mathematician and wrote books.

My sister Sheila was a very successful primary school teacher and has a remarkable talent for writing yards of rhyming verse on local subjects, much of which has been published.

Miriam's son Billy Keylock and his wife Cassie emigrated to Australia and became well established there, bringing up a large family.

Bill Coal's daughter Mavis became a college lecturer in domestic science.

Auntie Gwen's grandson Roger went to Oxford and wrote an acclaimed book about Africa.

My eldest daughter Jennifer is a Principal Educational

Psychologist with an autism charity, attending conferences worldwide.

My middle daughter Penelope is a Citizens Advice Bureau Advisor.

My youngest daughter Veronica owns and manages a 50-acre wood and is in the middle of bringing up three bright children.

And so it goes…

FURTHER NOTE

Long after the strikes of 1921 and 26, Wales suffered again from the 1984 miners strike and the obliteration of the coal fields. Scargill was right when he predicted that over 40 pits would go. But the working class cannot be obliterated, and neither can Socialism. When I went to newly independent Mozambique I found that it was a Portuguese-speaking country. Did the spirit of my great grandfather Martin Goldsworthy lean across the century and sympathise as I struggled to master that unfamiliar language?

Até logo,

Eva Goldsworthy, Llanfyllin, 2009.